Writing for the Market

Patricia O'Reilly

MERCIER PRESS

To my father

Mercier Press
PO Box 5, 5 French Church Street, Cork
24 Lower Abbey Street, Dublin 1

A CIP record for this book is available from the British Library.

ISBN 1 85635 130 3

    10   9   8   7   6   5   4   3   2   1

Typeset by Richard Parfrey in Lucida Bright and Helvetica Bold
Printed in Ireland by ColourBooks Ltd. Baldoyle, Dublin 13

Contents

Foreword

'Skill without imagination is craftsmanship.'

Tom Stoppard

The professional writer usually depends on skill and technique rather than luck or imagination. Skill and technique can be acquired and, when applied correctly, result in craftsmanship. To my knowledge, nobody has ever discovered a way to cultivate either luck or imagination.

I hope *Writing for the Market* will be a trigger for your craftsmanship and will help you to develop the professionalism that is as essential for success in the writing business as it is in any other business. Firmly subscribing to the theory that knowledge is power, this books aims to provide you with the information to enable you to write for and be published in today's market.

While some of the material here is culled from my own experience, the best is drawn from an eclectic cross-section of writers, some household names, others moderately famous, still others complete beginners – all willing to share their experiences generously and enthusiastically. Commissioning editors, publishers and radio producers were unstinting in detailing their requirements. The people interviewed were chosen with the aim of giving a flavour of the Irish market, rather than a comprehensive overview. What is certain is that there are considerable opportunities for the writer who tailors work to meet market requirements.

The growth of interest in writing is phenomenal, the talent incredible. During the many courses I've given, the same questions recur: where to get ideas; how and in what medium to write them; how to present copy; how to approach an editor/publisher/producer; when to follow up. In other words, how to write for the market. *Writing for the Market* was written to answer those questions.

At the end of a session I often ask individuals what they've achieved. The answers are as varied as the people and their aspirations. They range from the experiential: 'I have been published'; 'I've learned by doing'; 'I don't take rejection personally'; to the imaginative: 'The spark that lit the flame of my writing'; 'My writing is a key to escape the prison of self-imposed limitation'; to the practical: 'Involvement in group activity has focused my writing'; 'Writers write – I now write'; 'A world of communication has been opened from my home.'

Writing is the most exciting and exacting discipline of all. Enjoy it and write well. I hope this book, which cannot claim to be exhaustive or comprehensive because of confines of space, proves of great use to you.

This book could not have been written without the help of those who gave so generously of their knowledge, expertise and time. Thanks to the writers, researchers, students, publishers, editors RTE, BBC and local radio producers, too numerous to mention individually. A special thanks to the NUJ for supplying the information on which much of Chapter 3 is based, and to Catherine Murphy of Telecom Éireann.

1 Getting Going

A man may write at any time if he will set himself doggedly to it.

Samuel Johnson

General

The aim of *Writing for the Market* is to show you how and what to write for today's market. To accomplish this, as well as focusing on the technique of writing, we'll be analysing today's market and showing you how to tailor your writing to suit its requirements. All the areas of writing covered in this book have viable commercial outlets in Ireland and elsewhere. These include, for print: features, short stories, fiction and non-fiction books, and, for radio: talks, short stories, documentaries and plays. Because of the opportunities offered to new writers of radio plays and short stories, we'll also be looking at the requirements of BBC Radio Four.

'Talent alone cannot make a writer,' said Ralph Waldo Emerson more than a hundred years ago. And how right he was. While talent does help – it's a useful commodity in all fields of life – success in writing, particularly writing for which you will be paid, depends mostly on market analysis and commitment to satisfying market requirements.

It is often said that within every Irish person there's a book waiting to be released. Perhaps, but not all of us aspire to books. Maybe the captive is a short story, a play or, for those with a more practical turn of mind, a newspaper or a magazine feature. Or perhaps radio is your love. This book shows you how to handle each of these possibilities from initial inspiration through practical implementation to professional conclusion. In the process we'll debunk many of the current theories and prove to you that successful writing for today is 95 per cent knowledge, technique and discipline.

Think of a feature, story or play that appealed to you. Now pause and examine it a little more deeply. Chances are it's a topic with which you identified, that you're interested in and maybe even know something about. Also it's likely to have been presented in a style of writing with which you were comfortable, perhaps similar to your own. If it's not the way you write, don't worry; professional style can be acquired and indeed accomplished writers, as well as having their own individual style, can also emulate house style.

Consider carefully where the writer might have got the information and the way that information was compiled. Could you do it? Would you do it differently? In what way? If it has international overtones could it be tailored to the Irish market? It's only by exploring the various options that you'll realise the endless possibilities.

If it's a newspaper feature, could you envisage it adapted and expanded to a magazine feature? Which magazine do you think it might suit? (Next time you're buying a magazine, choose one that you feel you could and would like to write for.) Could your piece be the kernel of a short story? Would it provide a plot, even a subplot in a novel? Maybe it could be incorporated into a play? Could it be adapted for radio? Is it a topic with general appeal?

Once you've explored the possibilities of even one small feature and followed them up by even the most basic market analysis, you're beginning to get the idea of writing for the market. And once you've set in motion an analytical train of thought, you'll be amazed at how possibilities present themselves. From now on read analytically, think laterally and keep publication in mind.

Many people have the urge to write but find that it is difficult to start – actually to get down to putting one word after another. Even long-time professionals will tell you that.

You're sitting at your desk (or the kitchen table) with more than a dozen sharply pointed pencils and a pad of virgin paper waiting to be written on; or you're poised over the keyboard, fingers at the alert, ready to take off. You have three hours. You had planned to write at least, say, a feature. We're starting with a feature, because features have their own discipline and can often provide the imaginative trigger for other forms of writing. Also the discipline of finding an idea, researching, interviewing, writing, professionally presenting, selling, negotiating, seeing it in print and being paid is a complete learning curve in itself. If you can do it once, you can do it again, as Anne Dempsey knows.

Anne Dempsey

Today Anne Dempsey is a successful writer. Open any of the

national papers or magazines and you're likely to see a feature with her byline. Her range extends from women's and social issues to property and profiling. More than two decades ago she started small: 'With an article describing the ups and downs of my first year with my first child. I submitted it to a woman's magazine and had it published,' she says. 'Over the next year, some articles were accepted, more rejected. I couldn't figure out why some made it and others didn't. It didn't occur to me that I had the right to contact a features editor and ask for an explanation.'

Anne took a distance learning course in freelance journalism with the London School of Journalism. 'I was interested in feature writing, as I felt this offered more scope to a maternal freelance who was unable to respond to a story with the immediacy news editors need,' she says. 'I learned that good writing is simple writing; but to write simply and economically is not easy, not a cop out, but in fact, needs skill and practice.'

She says the course was helpful in terms of marketing, with her tutor proving knowledgeable about freelance outlets in Ireland. After a few months, she was ready for 'the big time. Her project was to:

- identify a publication she felt she would like to write for
- study publications to get a feel for articles – subject matter, length, treatment
- identify an article she could write and felt would be suitable
- interview, if required
- write and submit to features editor

She targeted the *Irish Independent*, which had recently introduced a woman's page with a new young editor. The subject Anne identified was the enterprise of a young business-woman who was sourcing, recycling and selling Victorian clothes, a forerunner of the current popular second-hand thrift shops. 'We met and I interviewed her – it's debatable which of us was the more nervous,' says Anne. 'My husband photographed her as she modelled a selection of the clothes she sold. I wrote my story, and sent it, unsolicited, to the paper with a covering letter.'

Then came the waiting, which she describes as: 'A great silence falling upon the nation. I would rush out every morning to buy the paper, returning with dashed hopes. Then about a fortnight later, there was my story and my byline and our photograph. Down the years, many thousands of words later, I still get a faint glimmer of that first feeling of delight and triumph.'

Anne says the most satisfying aspect was that she had been given a formula that worked. And worked again. 'Over the next few weeks, I repeated the exercise, and sent in two other stories which were also used.' Then the editor phoned asking for ideas. 'Convinced I'd never get such a good chance again, I burnt the midnight oil typing out fifty feature ideas and my proposed treatment for each one. These included some stories that can still hit the headlines, such as surviving in student flatland, fee-paying versus "free" education; but others, like a profile of a flower arranger, today would be considered too soft-focused. Ten were commissioned and I never looked back.'

Many writers who started in features have made a successful

transition to other areas of writing. These include Deirdre Purcell who, as a feature writer with the *Sunday Tribune,* was responsible for some penetrating profiles of interesting and controversial Irish figures. After co-writing Gay Byrne's autobiography, she moved full-time into fiction. To date her work includes *A Place of Stones, That Childhood Country, Falling for a Dancer* and her latest, *Francey. Irish Times* assistant editor Eugene McEldowney recently published his favourably received first novel, *A Kind of Homecoming.* Again, Rose Doyle spent many years on the staff and freelance features trail – and still walks it – though because of the successful reception of *Images* and *Kimbay* her primary focus is now fiction. Hugo Hamilton was a feature writer with the *Irish Press* until he turned novelist. *Surrogate City, The Last Shot* and *The Love Test* (due out in January 1995) are modern novels set in Germany. For several years June Considine freelanced, writing newspaper and magazine pieces ranging from social issues to business before changing to children's books. She followed the fantasy of the three Luvenders books with *View from a Blind Bridge,* its sequel *The Glass Triangle* (published summer 1994), and to date has published seven Beachwood novels.

But you don't need to come the journalistic/feature-writing route to be a writer. Christine Dwyer Hickey didn't.

Christine Dwyer Hickey

For years Christine Dwyer Hickey says she had been running away from her urge to write. After all she had a husband,

three children and a family business, more than a full-time
commitment! A broken shoulder after a riding accident in
1991 was the catalyst that set her going. She won the
Listowel Writers' Week short story competition in 1992 and
1993 and a special *Observer* award in 1993 with 'Teatro la
Fenice'.

'I had so many different ideas I decided to spread them
out into short stories rather than write a hysterical first
novel.' She bought two lined copybooks and set herself a
writing time of one hour a day for three months. 'I wrote
anything – the first few pages were such embarrassing
rubbish. Then came a sentence that sounded all right. My
first story was bad. My second was better and it actually had
a shape. And I just continued,' she says.

'One day I wrote a story about the Phoenix Park Race-
course, where I'd spent a lot of time as a child. Once I got
the first paragraph out, "Across the Excellent Grass" wrote
itself in one sitting and there were very few corrections.' That
was the story that won Listowel, followed the next year by
'Bridie's Wedding'. 'Month's Mind' was made into a TV film,
No Better Man, starring Niall Toibin and was broadcast on
RTE I in the autumn of 1993. Several follow-up scripts are
currently under consideration by RTE. *The Dancer*, Christine
Dwyer Hickey's first book, is due out in 1995. 'I keep my
writing very private, between myself and the page. The good
thing about writing is that nothing in your life goes to waste,
things always come back out on the page. I advise people
starting out to get a copybook, stop making excuses and
write all they can. I don't edit as I work but when I've
finished, I edit ruthlessly and objectively as though I'm

somebody else. I've graduated to a word processor, but I still use pen and paper when stuck.'

Sitting waiting for inspiration isn't the easiest way to go about writing. Before you start, it's best to have an idea at least of your theme, what you want to write about. New-comers are intimidated by research and interviewing, but as you'll realise it's often the easiest way to start. But more about that later on.

If you're going for the 'cold approach', that is, waiting for this rather nebulous inspiration to strike and it doesn't, try skim-reading a newspaper, a magazine or short story. If none of these inspires you, what's to be done? Well the first thing is stay put. Don't be tempted to make another cup of coffee, take the dog for a walk or ring your favourite cousin. This is your baptism of fire.

Begin with what the professionals call stream of consciousness writing – James Joyce was a master of the technique. This simply means, as Christine Dwyer Hickey says, putting down on paper the first thing that comes into your head, be it a word or a sentence, following it by the second and so on. It may take a few sheets of paper, it may take up to half an hour, but perseverance does pay, and out of what you often perceive to be confusion emerges the germ of an idea that can ultimately be incorporated into a feature or a short story. If nothing else, by actually writing you'll have broken the deadlock, loosened up and got flowing.

If you are a newcomer to writing who has, however, a knowledge of and a passion, say, for gardening, vintage cars, yachts, Egyptian culture, education...if you're an expert in it and know how and where to update your information, present it professionally and know where to submit copy, the chances are you'll be published. Starting like this is one of the easiest ways to get your name in print. But for most topics, unless you've a veritable library on the subject – and one that is constantly updated – you'll need to know where and how to do research.

Research venues

Research is one of the most important aspects of writing. (The list below is by no means complete – just a few basic pointers to start you off). Research consists simply of:
* Knowing where to acquire the relevant information
* Compiling a contact book for access to the appropriate professionals.

Information can be acquired from
* The relevant *Golden Pages* under your topic – a surprisingly useful and under-utilised jump-off point for information
* Libraries, some of which are listed below
  Corporation and County Council Libraries are listed under 'Libraries' in the relevant Golden Pages. Particularly useful is the Gilbert Library, 138 Pearse Street, Dublin tel 01-677 7662 and The Ilac Library, Dublin. Tel (01) 873 3996.
* Universities and many of the RTCs have research facilities, but you'll probably need a reading card. It's best to make a telephone enquiry in advance.

- Trinity College Library, Dublin. Tel (01) 677 2941. TCD, entitled to claim a copy of every book published within Ireland and the UK, currently has in excess of 3.5 million books, also CD ROM research databases on a variety of specific subjects. Access is strictly controlled. Members of the general public wishing to carry out research are recommended to make enquiries on Saturday mornings; undergraduates require a letter of introduction from their college.

- The National Library of Ireland in Kildare Street, Dublin. Tel (01) 661 8811. This is the *crème de la crème* for historical matters. Seating is limited so would-be researchers are encouraged to use their local library if material is available. Telephone for details on readers' tickets and readers' tickets for the manuscript room.

- Mercer Library and Beaumont Hospital Library cannot be beaten for researching matters medical. Facilities available include *Medline* on CD ROM; *Index Medicus*; *Current Contents* on Diskette; access to over 500 databases, with online searches carried out by trained library staff. A letter of introdution is required. For information ring Royal College of Surgeons in Ireland, Dublin 2. Tel (01) 478 0200.

- Central Catholic Library, Dublin 2. Tel (01) 676 1264. Specialists in philosophy, religion and social history. Currently the library has 400 runs of periodicals, 70,000 volumes, and if you ring in advance specifying your requirements, preliminary groundwork will be carried out. To become a member requires a standard application form, plus a guarantor.

- The Chester Beatty Library, Dublin. Tel: (01) 269 2386. The reference library includes manuscripts and scrolls of Chinese, Japanese, Burmese, Biblical, Arabic, Tibetan and Mongolian origin. Apply for research facility to director.
- The Irish Architectural Archive, Dublin 2. Tel (01) 6763430. Anyone wishing to research matters archit- ectural is welcome.
- Law Library, Dublin 7. Tel (01) 872 0622. Open only to members of the bar.
- State-of-the-art research facilities from RTE. Tel: (01) 208 3356/7:

  Eiresearch is a personal phone-in information service available during office hours, with assured confidentiality and turnaround no longer than three hours. A researcher accesses on-line databases including *Profile*. Information also sourced from *The Irish Times* index, built up over twenty-five years, subject specific and retrospective and from RTE's biographically-strong reference library. Subscription, £700 per annum, £200 per quarter, £50 per hour, includes photocopying, postal and fax charges

  Irish News Information Service (INIS) covers the main Irish daily and Sunday newspapers from 1 January 1994. Access to indexes and images of the newspaper articles is through software and a modem, installed on PC by RTE. Payment covers time on-line and per article viewed.
- NUJnet, the National Union of Journalists' electronic communications service for members, accessed by modem, costs approximately £4 per month, of which £1 is credited against usage. Facilities include looking up

information in on-line databases, sending telexes, filing copy direct to publications' computers. The network also includes announcements of jobs and contracts. Further information from NUJnet, Acorn House, 314 Gray's Inn Road, London, WCIX.

• State and semi-state bodies, banks and big businesses can be helpful mines of information.

Research material

When you're researching use a notebook or, if you're lucky enough to have them, a laptop or electronic notebook; or photocopy – the facility is available for a small charge in the majority of research venues. A rule of thumb is that for every 1,000 words you're going to write on a subject with which you're not familiar, you need in the region of 5,000 words of research.

Research is heady and exciting. Be ruthless about keeping to your primary focus. Be careful you aren't lured down blind alleys of interesting information. Resist the urge to delve into minor points and minor characters. Researching the architecture and furnishings of the Victorian era for a fairly long feature on a socialite of the time, I got carried away. I became such a mine of information on the history of fitted carpets, exercise horses, plate warmers and boudoirs that I almost forgot my commission was a historical profile.

When you're beginning your writing career concentrate on researching, writing and selling one piece at a time. But do make a note of any other feature ideas you stumble across during research.

The research information you acquire invariably shapes the article. At this point it must be said that stubborn determination to use every scrap of research material you have unearthed, relevant or not, can ruin a good feature. What you leave out is as important as what you include. It won't be wasted. Keep it. Its value in the future, if used properly, will more than reward your restraint. Never be content with writing just one or two pieces about a topic when your research will keep you funded to sell different angles on your subject to different papers, trade, specialist, magazines and overseas. The main problem, as you'll discover in wringing research dry, is that you'll get tired of the subject, be delighted to see the back of it and move on to pastures new.

An excellent beginner, full of ideas, had a feature editor interested in a piece to run on 14 October 1993, the two-hundredth anniversary of the day Marie Antoinette was guillotined. So carried away did he get with research, however, and so much did he accumulate that he was unable to marshal the relevant facts to make the required 600-word feature. And he missed his chance.

Notebook

A writer's notebook is a most vital piece of equipment. Into it you can jot down facts, ideas, quotations, useful and useless bits of information, colourful phrases, snatches of thoughts, lines of dialogue, moods, emotions. It comes into its own when inspiration is just not flowing. You can use your imagination to start reaction between apparently unrelated ideas. Be curious about human motives, error, love and hatred; and people – the way they look, the clothes they choose, the environment they create; watch body language, social interaction; consider the books people read, their vocal mannerisms. Listen to conversations, eavesdrop unashamedly. Note down things you hear, sentences you read, snatches of dialogue that appeal to you, quotable quotations. Pieces like these spark off one another and, fuelled by the imagination, trigger ideas. A page of your notebook could read something like the following:

House: a cavernous depot for the storage of marital silences

Call money: money at call and at short notice

Double income dinner parties

Dancing: the vertical expression of horizontal desire

For all her thinness she had a breakfast cereal air of health, a soap-and-lemon cleanness.

He bent his head at every step and seemed to be continually bowing.

Window shopping: parading up and down a shopping street with intent to covet rather than to buy

If we end up together, this is the most romantic day of my life. If we don't I'm a slut.

Beautiful young people are accidents of nature. Beautiful old people create themselves.

A sound of low fugitive laughter

Contact book

From the beginning of your writing career it is a good idea to start a contact book. Writers often need fast access to accurate professional information. A list of contacts could include a banker, solicitor, psychologist, psychiatrist, architect, stockbroker, a few socialites, fundraisers, perhaps an interior designer, the selection dependent on the theme of your writing.

When you're building up that contact book, do make a note of the names, titles and telephone numbers of the various people you talk to. Many professional writers will cross reference name with subject, i.e. suppose your architect is named John Barry, duplicate under A and B.

Using your contact book

We all know courtesy goes a long way, but often in the heat and excitement of acquiring information it can be forgotten. If you are looking for information over the phone be clear about what you want to ask or, preferably, have your questions already written down. Check that the time is suitable for your contact to talk to you. If they agree, explain what you're doing and ask the relevant questions. Check that you may use their name; get their approval to quote them. Unless you are absolutely sure, check the spelling of their name and title. Finally, if you're writing on a subject with which you're not completely *au fait*, it's a good idea to ask your informant to check finished copy. If your contact is busy or your call inconveniently timed, ask for a convenient time and ring back on the dot. If your contact is reluctant to be quoted or to give information, so be it. Find someone else.

Interview techniques

The purpose of interviews is to elicit clear and comprehensible information from the interviewee. Short interviews, quotations and comments can be successfully done over the phone but longer ones and profiles are best carried out face to face.

Before you make contact, know what information you require. Prior to interview do your research and have a list of questions prepared. But don't take even printed material as gospel. Check again name spelling and title.

Your approach will be dictated by the type of interview and the occasion and can vary greatly even with the same person. If you were interviewing the Minister of Agriculture, your handling and questions would vary depending on whether your focus is the government's EC policy, the minister's favourite book, his attitude to corporal punishment, or as the neighbour of a family which suffered a tragedy.

One of the most important factors in interviewing is making your interviewees feel relaxed and ensuring they trust you enough to talk freely. Do dress for the occasion: if you're interviewing a pinstripe-suited captain of industry wear a suit but if you're seeing a student, jeans will be fine. When talking, make eye-contact and use the person's name frequently. A professional (and usually successful ploy) is to take interviewees into your confidence by asking their opinion on the programme or the publication in question, discussing where this piece fits in, mentioning others you may have already interviewed, indicating your *modus operandi* and some of the topics you propose to cover. Before finishing, check if there is anything your interviewee would like to add and ask if there are any other areas you should look at. This is paying a courtesy by recognising expertise on the subject and from your own point of view, it could open the valve to your most valuable information.

Venue is important. If possible go to the interviewee, whether at the office or home. The success of *Hello* and similar publications is based on reporters and photographers bringing to their readers the rich and the famous in their own homes. Choice of colour schemes, books, flowers, paintings, furnishings are very telling. Equally, offices can reveal a lot about their occupants: austere, paperless, steamlined offices tend to belong to one type of person, whereas those who function in a jumble of overflowing bookshelves and desks piled high with papers have a different attitude to life. If your interview is taking place in the office, try and get your subject to come out from behind the desk – if nothing else, it forms a psychological barrier.

Interviews can be taped, which guarantees accuracy and allows you to make regular eye contact, but do watch out for unfamiliar words and make sure to check spelling (best done between questions). You can use shorthand, but that does require more concentration on notebook than subject and again you've to clarify unfamiliar names/terms. Or you can just make notes of key trigger words and dates – ideal if you're an experienced interviewer. One of the simplest ways to do this is to do this is to circle your main focus point in the centre of the page and to run from it second, third and fourth spurs, as necessary.

Interviews usually fall into four categories:

- Expert (scientist, architect, academic, etc)
- Political (politician, union leader, spokesperson, etc)
- Personality (writer, actor, entertainer, etc)
- Human Interest (bank-robbery/car-accident witness, parents whose child has been killed, farmer whose land is flooded)

Pre-interview preparation is vital. The questions to ask yourself include:

- Who am I interviewing?
- About what?
- For what reason?

When compiling your questions keep them simple and direct. Know the information you want and look for the answers for it. Find out if the interviewee has previously written or spoken about the subject. Check that your background research is correct.

The commandments of interviewing include:

- Being confident and at ease with yourself. If you're not, it won't inspire your interviewee
- Doing your homework, knowing your topic and your interviewee as well as you can
- Keeping questions concise, direct and to the point
- Listening to the answers. If you don't understand them, will your reader?
- Choosing your interviewing technique according to the

type of interview and the nature of the topic

Some questions to be asked at interview – particularly useful
if you're looking for the person behind the public persona –
but do tailor them to suit the occasion:

- What is the quality you most like in a person?
- What is your idea of perfect happiness?
- What talent would you most like to have?
- What is the trait you most deplore in others?
- What is your most treasured possession?
- What is your greatest extravagance?
- On what occasion do you lie?
- What is your favourite journey?
- What do you dislike about your appearance?
- Which living person do you most admire?
- Which living person do you most despise?
- When and where were you happiest?
- What is your most marked characteristic?
- Who is your favourite hero of fiction?
- What do you regard as the lowest depth of misery?
- Who are your favourite writers?
- What do you value in your friends?
- If you could choose what to come back as after death,
  what would it be?
- What is your motto?
- What is your birth sign?
- Favourite piece of music/book/food/place?

Tools of the trade

Word Processor

Without doubt, the most vital tool of trade for any writer has become the word processor. It makes writing better and faster. You can create, check and change your text on screen before printing out. Indeed it is so easy to revise text that the difficulty is stopping. Remember too much editing can remove the 'soul' from a piece. Once you've stored text it need not be keyed again, even by the typesetter, and an increasing number of newspapers, magazines and publishers are requesting text on disk, as well as in hard copy. The modem (short for *mo*dulator and *dem*odulator) allows research material and copy to be transmitted and received via telephone from and on to screen and is becoming another vital piece of equipment for the get-ahead writer.

The type of computer that runs a word processor is known as a microcomputer, desktop or laptop computer. It includes a keyboard, the computer 'box' and the screen (VDU or monitor). The word-processing software is usually bought separately. There are more than 500 different types of word processing software available. Among those recommended for writers are Word, WordStar and Word Perfect. All word processing packages are competent and they share about 80 per cent of the same features.

One of the joys of working with a processor is WYSIWYG (What You See Is What You Get), which means that the layout shown on screen is the same as that produced on the paper. If you can afford it, buy a laser printer, the Rolls Royce of printers for quality and speed; or an Inkjet printer for the Mac which produces laser-quality printouts, at a slower rate, for a fraction of the cost.

Many of us writers – something to do with right and left brain dominance, creativity versus practicality – have a reluctance, not only to keep abreast with electronic technology but even to have anything to do with it. But if we want to write for today's market, our future lies with this high technology and whether or not we understand it, we will be able to use it. The majority of us learned to drive a car. And we can, with even the minimum of perseverance, master a processor, an answering machine and a fax. While we don't need to understand the inner technical details to be able to write and present proficient copy, it is a good idea to buy from a dealer in a convenient location and to negotiate a suitable package of price and help. This equipment is not wildly expensive and the even better news is that the price if all this gadgetry is coming down fast.

Telephone answering machine

This device has become invaluable, particularly if you choose one that allows you to pick up your messages when away from your workplace. It has the benefits of a mobile phone, in that you are never too long out of contact, but it does allow you control of returning calls and is much less intrusive.

Fax

In these days of instant communication and escalating telephone charges, the facsimile or fax, as it is more colloquially known, is fast becoming another vital piece of equipment. This allows exact duplicates of documents, whether handwritten, line-drawn or typeset, to be transmitted over telephone lines. Today's faxes can produce an image detailed enough to do justice to a photograph.

These aids give us the freedom to work where and when we choose, to send material in hard copy or on a floppy disk, or to transmit it direct to publisher by fax or by modem.

On the subject of where we work: masterpieces have been written in snatched minutes, on the corner of the kitchen table, in a parked car. Jackie Collins, writing sister of actress Joan and author of *The Stud* and *Hollywood Wives,* wrote in longhand while waiting to collect her children from school. Barbara Cartland, queen of romantic fiction, dictates from the comfort of a chaise-longue. But if possible, opt for a more formal approach. Pick your own place, be it a corner where you can site your desk or a whole study or office. It's easier to be serious about writing when you adopt a professional approach and have to hand your reference books, dictionary, thesaurus, and a desk that will remain undisturbed.

How long should you work? At the beginning, research, compilation and polishing take longer. Remember you're finding your feet, learning, gaining invaluable experience. So take it easy, but write regularly and rejoice in your accomplishments. A perfect nugget of a paragraph is work well done. The majority of professionals either write at full tilt when working on a project, or else do a certain number of words each day (seeming to vary between 1,000 to 5,000) both polished and unpolished. The consensus is that writing for, say, three hours may not steadily advance work, whereas precise wordage does.

2 Newspaper Features

Newspapers always excite curiosity.

Charles Lamb

Finding a feature

For the purpose of *Writing for the Market* we're using features as the bridge between news journalism and creative writing and as a jump-off for many of the other media forms.

So what's the difference between news stories, features and creative writing? News stories report the news, are written factually usually in house style, with the essence of the story contained in the first paragraph and developed without frills in subsequent paragraphs. Many features are triggered by news stories.

For instance the news on the front page of the national dailies at the beginning of the summer of 1994 of the new legislation giving gardai the power to arrest battering husbands on the spot spawned several features on different aspects of violence in the home. Some took the form of interviews with battered wives; others analysed the husbands who did the battering; more looked at the support group Move (Men Overcoming Violence).

Public interest in domestic violence was further fuelled

by the screening on RTE 1 around the same time of Roddy Doyle's *Family*. Set in a deprived area of Dublin, it was a bleak four-part story of marital breakdown from the perspective of a different family member in each episode.

The majority of newspaper and magazine features, inspired by news stories but with further information required to flesh out the original spine, do stand or fall on detailed research and interviewing, interesting facts and clear stylish writing.

Creative writing is fiction. An apt description of fiction is, 'fact laced with fantasy'. Back to using facts that can originate in a news story, develop into a feature and end up as a work of fiction.

Analyse the best stories, plays and books and you'll see that the majority have what is called a topic. Violence in the home is a politically correct topic for the 1990s, as are AIDS, career women, interior design. Most topics, along with the right characters, location and conflict, can be the ingredients of fiction, which brings us to the learning curve towards creative writing that is provided by features.

Take a look at any of our daily, Sunday, evening or local papers. As well as both home and international news coverage, there will be several features. Some are written by staff members but increasingly they will be by freelance writers. More freelance feature material comes into the average newspaper office than any other sort of freelance copy. The space allocated to feature material is determined by newspaper size and the amount of space given over to advertisements and news. The former brings in revenue; news and features have to be paid for.

A features editor, if approached by a freelance in the proper manner, will usually listen to an idea. The exceptions can be if it is in-house policy to have features written by staff, if the budget allocation for outside contributors is tight or if it is totally an NUJ (National Union of Journalists) house, as is the case with some of the national papers. The last means that only paid-up members of the NUJ will be published. To become a member of the NUJ, the bulk of your income, that is, at least two-thirds of your total earned income, must be derived from journalism.

You've a better chance of interesting a commissioning editor if you tie your feature to a topical news issue, such as the change in gardai legislation referred to above. For instance a feature on a divorce referendum, property tax, cut in educational budget, an exclusive profile of a snooker star around the time of the world championships or an advance telephone interview with somebody famous coming to Ireland has a better chance of succeeding than a non-specific idea. Always keep your senses tuned into feature opportunities. It's surprising how often they come up.

One of my most unexpected stories turned up several years ago while I was spending a weekend with my family in London. Wandering through Covent Garden we happened on Sue Townsend signing copies of *The Secret Diary of Adrian Mole*. A colourful, bubbly, obliging lady, she gave a quick interview and made arrangements for her publisher to send on biographical details. I sold the piece to *The Irish Times* to run a few days before RTE's screening of her television series.

Again on another family holiday in Dingle, we stayed in

the same hotel as country and western singer, Dolly Parton, who enchanted staff and guests alike with her delight in everything. A bonus was that the hotel was perched on the headland below which Fungi, the now world-famous bottle-nosed dolphin, did his cavorting each morning. Between Dolly Parton and Fungi it was a financially rewarding week as well as being a great holiday.

There are all sorts of possible features:
- Business, i.e. company and personal profiles of our captains of industry, market analysis, specific analysis
- Advertising features, which are becoming an increasingly important source of revenue for newspapers and require a special journalistic skill of balancing the reality and the information the company or person wants presented to the public
- Sporting features, which can range from profiles to history of clubs and sporting events
- Fashion, beauty, women's issues and increasingly men's issues

The options and variations of subject for features open to the innovative writer are endless. Certain topics come around with faithful regularity. These include:
- Education, which can be tied into starting school in September, college in October, uniforms, the cost of books, stress, both parental and student, the Junior Cert, the Leaving Cert, study patterns, graduation, the debs' ball
- Christmas – parties with a difference, innovative presents, dealing with hangovers, decorating the house, the most expensive or economical wrappings

- St Valentine's Day, Mother's Day, Father's Day
- Anniversaries – famous people who were born, accomplished something specific or died within the calendar year – all grist to the feature writer's mill

Regulars that can be trotted out include stress and depression, men, women, incest, abortion, child abuse, housing, unemployment, divorce, the elderly, the young, the poor, travelling people, men with beards, bald men, blonde women, redheads, tanning, dieting, career versus home, house husbands. As you can see the list is infinitely wide and almost any subject, given an innovative angle, the right treatment and the appropriate market chosen is publishable. There is nothing more pointless than to offer to, say, the editor of a sailing magazine a piece on ingrown toenails!

Selling an idea

So you have an idea and you are ready to approach the features editor of the newspaper or magazine of your choice, having first made sure that your subject and the publication you have in mind are compatible and that you have the facts at your fingertips.

- Get the name of the features editor.
- Ask if he/she is interested in outside contributions. (You will usually be answered in the affirmative.)
- Sell your idea succinctly and with enthusiasm.
- You'll likely be asked to present either a proposal or the feature.
- If a proposal, respond immediately in bullet point form.

- If a completed feature is required, check:
    writing format, i.e. interviews, focus or other
    when you'll have verdict
    required wordage
    deadline
- On acceptance, make sure you'll have a byline; find out publication date, payment (If necessary, do point out length of time spent on research.) and date of payment.
- If your feature is not accepted, immediately go through the motions with another suitable publication.
- Remember it's only you who can sell your idea.

Breaking into a national daily

Often fact can be stranger than fiction and a dream can come true even in the cynical world of newspapers. Carol knows. It happened to her.

While researching for her thesis, which was on *The Diet Industry and Body Image*, Carol came across *Yes*, an English magazine aimed at the larger lady, focusing on clothes, exercise that promoted fitness not weight loss, but above all presenting the large woman in a positive light which up to now was not the norm. There was an article about 'International No Diet Day', a one day moratorium based on celebrating what you are, ditching that diet and getting on with living. The piece was written by the founder of the day, Mary Evans Young, who explained where the idea came from and went through its history to date. This was its third year.

Carol, who was looking for a break into features, felt she

could be on a winner. She made a few preliminary enquiries to find out if the day was being celebrated in Ireland. Nobody knew anything about it. 'Being totally new to the business and somewhat naïve, I felt I wouldn't be able to break this story without help,' she says. 'So with a deadly combination of enthusiasm, excitement and perhaps impatience at having a "hot" story on my hands I phoned the Clare McKeon Show on FM 104, to which I'm a regular listener, and spoke to Clare herself. She was enthusiastic and agreed to do a show about it on the day itself – 5 May – provided her producer was in agreement.'

About a week later Carol delivered an information pack to the station containing all the facts about the day, extracts from a book, *Forbidden Body* by Shelley Bovey, giving examples of size prejudice, and a reading list. She had worked through the night to put the pack together and kept her fingers crossed until four days later she got confirmation that the show was going ahead.

'Meanwhile I had been waiting for a more detailed information pack from Mary Evans Young, but due to problems with the postal system, I still had not received it – in fact, I never got it,' she says. 'Time was running out so I phoned Mary, who then faxed me an up-to-date press release. I also got some background information on Mary herself. So with my press release, background information and the magazine article, I spent the weekend writing a feature about the day.'

On Monday Carol approached one of the Dublin dailies, gave it the first three paragraphs and a covering letter requesting confirmation of acceptance or refusal by the following Wednesday. By now it was only a week to No Diet

Day. She phoned the paper on the Wednesday. They turned the story down. She then rang the features editor of the another daily and offered him the story. He seemed interested and asked to see it, so she submitted the entire story to him early next morning, again asking for acceptance or rejection by the following day. That evening he phoned. He wanted to publish. A price was agreed and it was published on 4 May, the day before No Diet Day.

On the same day the story was accepted, a PR company that was connected to the radio show approached Carol. They planned to have a media launch for No Diet Day in a restaurant owned by one of their clients and wanted Carol to turn over to them her information and to help with the launch. 'Initially I agreed, but on second thoughts I decided not to. As I had spent so much time, incurred a certain amount of expense and done all the work, I felt reluctant to part with any information. I could not figure how I stood to gain from the launch, as the PR company was unwilling to pay me for my services,' says Carol.

Finally 5 May arrived. To her surprise, when Carol got up that morning and turned on 2FM, she heard Gerry Ryan talking about her feature. 'It gave me a great boost. I later learned that I would have been on his show had his researcher been able to get in touch with me. She phoned the newspaper that published me, but the person she spoke to didn't have my telephone number.'

The Clare McKeon Show went out at 6pm and Carol was to give her view on air by telephone. She was introduced as the first woman to bring No Diet Day to Ireland (true!) and her feature of the previous day was discussed. Just before

Carol was due to go on she was told that Mary Evans Young, whom she had booked to take part, was not available and that she would have to explain No Diet Day to the listeners. 'This threw me off balance a little and when I went on my mind went blank. I recovered and made sense, but I was relieved to be off air.'

The show was deemed a success. Pat Henry, gym owner who promotes regular exercise and a healthy diet, and comedienne Jo Brand gave their views. The listeners who phoned in were thrilled to have No Diet Day and discussed how they felt about body image and weight problems.

So what happened afterwards? Carol says she has had people asking her for more information and urging her to do a follow-up.

One woman who counsels people with eating disorders thanked her for bringing the story to the media, saying the more discussions and features on eating disorders the better, as she didn't feel it was a subject being taken seriously in Ireland. Carol was approached by the same PR company offering her freelance writing work should it become available; FM 104 have asked her to keep in touch; the daily that published her requested more features and commissioned her to interview Jo Brand.

'However, the main benefit I received was the practical experience of writing and selling the feature. I learned not to underestimate or undervalue my work and skills. I came to the realisation that having a story works both ways – you're doing them a favour as much was they're doing you one,' says Carol.

Making it in the provincials

'My experiences with the provincial papers have been frustrating on one hand, yet successful and extremely enjoyable on the other,' says Kevin, who lives in rural Ireland and is determined to 'make it' in newspapers. 'But they have served as an invaluable learning process.'

For over two years he had been a regular sports contributor – in the unpaid club column of a local paper. 'I wanted to start writing as a journalist for this newspaper and I've succeeded.'

'Personally I think the day of written application alone for employment has long since gone. I approached the deputy editor at a local function one Sunday afternoon. I presented myself as Kevin – he remembered me from one of my previous applications – and asked him if I could cover a function in my home town the following Thursday. I was amazed when he agreed, but thanked him for his co-operation.'

Never one to let the grass grow under his feet and constantly tuned into opportunity, before leaving that afternoon Kevin asked if he could write a report on the function they were both attending. 'Acknowledging my brave impudence, he looked at me and half smiled. 'I'd like you to,' he answered. Amazed, yet again, I did. The sense of fulfilment on seeing my byline on the stories was phenomenal'.

Then Kevin, for many years a cinema buff, turned his hand to film reviews by writing up the next two movies he saw. He is now the paper's cinema reviewer – with free and immediate access to the latest films.

He insists he's not suggesting that originality always pays off. But he does say he has been lucky in other aspects also. 'My Sunday afternoons are spent delving through the papers – about eight of them. Then magic! Being presumptuous, I started a weekly column on 'What the Sunday Papers Said'. After all, I might as well put them to further use. Yes, I was successful. In addition I regularly produce 'News Week in Review' columns. These are just simple ideas.

His tips for wannabee writers is succinct and in character. 'Don't limit your abilities. Arrange payment before writing. You'll have spent time and effort on your article, not to mention expense. Make sure you receive what you deserve. If one of your ideas doesn't work, try another.'

Beginners, especially, should beware of exploitation. We have heard stories of people's ideas being taken up, only to appear in a newspaper a few weeks later under someone else's byline, and of freelance contributions being accepted and published but only on the basis of no payment at all. Look out for yourself, and remember, your work is worthy of proper payment.

Requirements of newspaper features editors

The basic requirements of the newspaper editors we spoke to were factual accuracy, professional compilation and presentation, and correct spelling and grammar. These are all skills which can be easily – well, relatively easily – acquired.

Cork Examiner Publications

The daily *Cork Examiner* is in the market primarily for news features based on topical news stories, preferably in the Munster area.

The focus of *Life Extra*, published midweek, is women's affairs, family issues and profiles, not necessarily Munster-based.

Weekender supplement carries property, books, fashion, profiles.

The *Evening Echo*, while more confined to Cork City, is interested in features of general interest written in an entertaining way.

'Preferably ring in with your idea,' says *Examiner* Features Editor, Dan Buckley. 'If we're interested, but don't know your work, you'll be asked to submit without commitment and we'll let you know as soon as possible. Do give us a contact number. But if you don't hear from us, you should follow up with a call within a few days. Another thing – we can't guarantee to return scripts, even if accompanied by an SAE. That's the reality of the newspaper business.'

He says his paper receives 'vast numbers of unsolicited features' and asks would-be contributors to bear in mind that most newspapers have staff reporters specialising in certain areas and there's little point in trying to break into those. 'Newcomers are in with a better chance of publication if they pitch material to stuff we wouldn't get from other sources, remembering that we're provincial but not parochial.' He says that pieces should be kept 'reasonably short', generally around the 800-word mark. 'Keep it tight; don't pad. If you make life difficult for an editor or a sub-editor, they won't want to know you.'

Dan Buckley's last piece of advice is that when contributors become regulars, they should supply their bank account number and sorting code for direct payment. 'They'll be paid more quickly.'

Independent Newspapers, publishing the *Irish Independent, Sunday Independent* and *Evening Herald*

Irish Independent Features Editor Gerry Mulligan says: 'We're absolutely in the market for freelance features. Give us a ring if you've just one idea. It's better still if you've two or three. A direct approach is best. By its nature journalism is about communication.' He says that by ringing in the would-be contributor gets an immediate decision, although a rough outline in writing may be requested to clarify ideas on illustrations, photography, artwork and so on. 'Time is of the essence. We like the immediate response. Be prepared to write and deliver within forty-eight hours.' He says that people ring in without knowing the newspaper business. 'There's not much point in somebody in Dublin trying to outdo somebody in Hollywood with a story about Hollywood. We want original ideas based in Ireland, stories with national appeal.' From Monday to Friday the *Independent* has two-

and-a-half pages for features, twelve on Saturday. The focus of 'Lifestyle' includes health, beauty, fitness, diet, coping, parenting. The General Features section deals with some very serious subjects, such as death from cystic fibrosis, some less serious, like the cost of car insurance. 'Be aware of the time of year. Topicality is important. There's no point in offering features on school during the summer.'

Anne Harris, Features Editor of the *Sunday Independent*, welcomes approaches from new writers. 'Unsolicited submitted material should only be testimony to the potential contributor's ability to write,' she says. 'I welcome a written list of ideas, including some subjects with immediate relevance. What I'm looking for is a piece of writing that's going to arrest my attention. If I found one lambent sentence in an unsolicited piece it would lift my spirits.' Anne Harris wants contributors to think visually as well as verbally, actually picturing the printed illustrated story.

Since the advent of electronic communication, she says she gets mountains of Faxed material. 'I look at all unsolicited copy and, if it is not suitable, try as a matter of policy to return it with a comment – obviously this is not always possible. Posted material properly presented does get more attention.'

Anne Harris says that many of the *Sunday Independent*'s freelances, such as Barry Egan, Brighid MacLaughlin, Molly McAnailly Burke, Patricia Redlich, Ciara Ferguson and Orla Healy, began as unknowns and have become household names. 'Freelances stay with us, which says everything. We give writers such as Terry Keane and Declan Lynch full scope to develop their unique talents.'

'We're unapologetically market-oriented and you can't be market-oriented without being concerned for standards and good journalism. We're not a crusading paper and don't take a high moral tone but we do fight for democracy and liberal values,' says Anne Harris. 'This is entirely compatible with good journalism.'

Evening Herald Features Editor David Robbins says that most features are supplied by staff or regular freelances and that they use very few unsolicited pieces. The paper is almost completely NUJ.

The Irish Times

Caroline Walsh, Features Editor, describes her relationship with freelances as symbiotic: 'We need you and you need us.' The paper uses graduates in journalism, some of whom end up on the staff, and favours NUJ members, but also nurtures new talents and specialists. 'When you start out,' says Caroline, 'the trick is to find the line between confidence and arrogance, between selling yourself and driving people crazy.' She says the newspaper business is about producing news and that would-be journalists must keep informed. 'Newspapers and radio are the briefing documents of the day. It's a necessary investment to buy the papers and listen to the news each morning. We live in a world that never ceases to throw up stories. Journalism is about knowing what's going on – being clued in, copped on and developing a curiosity.' *Irish Times* staff cover the mainstream stories of courts, politics. Freelances have to dig deeper and work harder, go for more subterranean, offbeat stories. 'I'll commission someone who comes up with a story I haven't thought of.' She favours ideas in writing, which she deals with as soon as possible, saying, 'While there's an immediacy in journalism, phone calls can come when you're on overload.' Her advice to the newcomer is to be aware that journalism is a competitive business and not to talk about an idea until it has been published.

Sunday Business Post

Features Editor Aileen O'Toole says, 'As 90 per cent of our material is generated in-house, we don't have as much of a need to source freelance material as other papers. We get a lot of approaches from freelances and, while we're not shutting the door, we don't have a massive budget and we're discriminating about the stories we buy in. We're more likely to commission a piece from an economist or an academic to link in with a news story.' In terms of approach, she prefers a letter. 'It's easier to gauge on paper whether it's a good idea, well thought-out, well structured, angled and specific rather than general, and it gives me the opportunity to guide the writer as to our requirements rather than have somebody spend time writing a story that's unlikely to be handled the way we want it.' She receives a lot of unsolicited material, 95 per cent of which is returned to the writer. The main flaws are: subject-matter not exciting; not in keeping with the market; has appeared elsewhere. 'We want exclusive news stories, at a new angle that will bring the story forward. With regard to features, we favour interview-based, non-judgemental pieces, lots of quotations, no fancy footwork creating a story that doesn't exist, a sense of style and a good standard of writing. While we're people-led, we're not interested in people who are too exposed in media terms.'

Sunday Press

Make contact either with Features Editor, Frances O'Rourke or Philip Nolan, Deputy Features Editor. 'By and large,' says Philip Nolan, 'We use copy from NUJ members, the main exception being people with specialist knowledge. 'The idea in writing is favoured rather than a telephone enquiry. Invariably you'll get a call at the wrong time.' The response will be fairly quick and if you get to write your feature, the preferred method of presentation is a one-paragraph 30-word summary. 'While most of our features are reactive (to news stories), topical ideas, such as D-Day anniversary coverage which was started in January 1994, are worked on months in advance. Anyone interested in covering anniversaries, for instance, should approach us well ahead of time.'

Northern Ireland dailies

Belfast Newsletter

This daily tabloid has a large circulation, particularly in east Ulster. Features Editor Geoff Hill will consider freelance contributions. He favours an exploratory letter rather than a complete submission and will tell you as soon as possible whether your idea is of interest to him.

Belfast Telegraph

Weekday daily and evening newspaper; this popular broadsheet includes features in such areas as lifestyle, personalities and entertainment. Features Editor Janet Devlin welcomes offers of freelance contributions but prefers to receive a letter in advance detailing the area you wish to write about, your qualifications, experience etc.

Irish News

Published daily in Belfast, this broadsheet's Features Editor is Colm McAlpine. Freelance pieces are considered on their merits. Prospective freelances should send a speculative letter in the first instance either to the Editor, Tom Collins or the Deputy Editor, Noel Doran.

3 Feature Facts

Writing is a dog's life, but the only one
worth living.

Gustave Flaubert

Conditions for freelance work

If you plan to be a regular contributor to newspapers in
particular – the majority of Irish magazines are not union
houses – you will need to become a member of the NUJ. The
basic requirement, as previously mentioned, is that two-
thirds of your earned income be derived from journalism.
The situation is rather a 'chicken-and-egg' one – it's difficult
to do regular newspaper work if you're not unionised and
yet you can't become a member until you do. But someone
who really wants to write features will not be fazed.

Here it must be noted that while the following are the ideal
conditions for freelances, they are seldom entirely adhered to
by the editors. Supply and demand are lopsided in the corridors
of journalism – i.e. each year there are more and more
journalists appearing and the majority start their career by
freelancing and usually with features. So it is a case of the
survival of the best and strongest. But remember that most
newspapers and magazines could not survive without a steady
input of work from freelance writers.

Commissions

A commission is a contract in law. It is a contract for services, not a contract of service (employment). It is normal business practice to agree terms and confirm them in writing before goods are delivered or services rendered. The editor or commissioning agent, when commissioning a freelance, should always state:

- the minimum rate to be paid
- a minimum length for written material
- arrangements for reimbursement of all expenses
- adequate specification of material to be published
- when payment is to be made and whether or not interest is attracted by late payments

A word-of-mouth contract is legally binding. But whenever possible, verbal agreements should be confirmed in writing. This can be done by:

- letter
- fax
- NUJ writers commissioning forms

Expenses

Expenses should be paid on at least the same basis as to staff, and should cover full subsistence, travel costs including car mileage as assessed by the AA, necessary entertainment, phone calls and other communications costs. Where freelances pay out these expenses and claim them back later, a handling charge of 10 per cent should be added. Where expenses are going to be a significant amount, perhaps on assignments involving expensive travel, ideally some agreement as to their likely level should be reached beforehand and a reasonable proportion paid in advance. This is the ideal situation – it seldom occurs.

Cancellation fee

If a commission has been cancelled before the work has been done, a cancellation or 'kill' fee of at least 50 per cent of the agreed fee should be paid. Once work has been supplied it should be paid for in full, whether or not it is published.

Copyright

According to Section 11 of the Copyright, Designs and Patents Act 1988 freelances automatically own the copyright of commissioned or speculatively submitted material. The editor acquires only those rights intended by both parties at the time of commissioning. In other words, an editor can acquire more than first rights in written material only with the agreement of the freelance and these rights are 'intellectual property' to be sold, not given away. The act stipulates that the freelance retains copyright on his or her work (unless there is an agreement to the contrary).

Here it must be stated that there is no copyright on ideas and the only protection for ideas is where they are stated to be confidential, imparted in confidential circumstances and are of commercial value. Therefore, all ideas, memos and synopses should be marked 'confidential'.

Speculatively offered material

The editor should inform the freelance whether speculatively offered material is accepted or rejected within two weeks of receipt. If he or she is unable to decide, a holding fee should be negotiated with the freelance. Acceptance should be confirmed in writing, stating the rights requested, the fees to be paid, any arrangements about expenses, and, in the case of written material, minimum length.

Payment should be made within one month of acceptance. If more material is published than originally intended, payment should be made for the outstanding amount by the end of the calender month following publication. Rejected material should be returned immediately. Again, *ideally* this is what should happen. It seldom does.

Brain-picking

Editors wishing to buy information from a freelance must do so at the same rate of payment as they buy features. No editor or staff journalist should expect to pick up back-ground information, contact numbers and so on from freelances without paying for it. But they do and can get narky if payment is mentioned. Memos supplied should be paid for at at least the equivalent news lineage rate.

Technology

There are still problems regarding satisfactory house agreements for freelances using new technology. The NUJ suggests that freelances asked to transmit copy electronically should note the following:

- Take advice from publications you work for on acquiring appropriate equipment and software.
- While some employers offer equipment and/or financial assistance, freelances are best advised to buy equipment which suits them and to recover costs by charging realistic fees.
- Resist keying in own copy in newspaper offices without extra payment.
- Issue clear invoices for electronically transmitted material, including not only fee for work, but also additional 'downloading' fee to cover costs of electronic equipment, self-training and transmission. Suggested level of this fee is 10 per cent of total charge for work involved, i.e. a job charged at £100 becomes £110.

Freelance checklist

- Make sure you clearly understand the requirements of the relevant feature editor.
- Record the names and positions of people you deal with

– particularly those responsible for payment.
- Confirm fees and conditions in writing.
- Follow up where necessary to confirm that material has arrived and is acceptable.
- Send an invoice as soon as possible – or confirm that an effective self-billing arrangement operates.
- Check that payment arrives as promised. If it doesn't, telephone to find out where it is.
- Keep records so you can see who owes you money and satisfy the revenue commissioners.

Presentation of newspaper features

Copy must be typed. The cardinal rule is double spacing on one side only of white A4 paper, allowing wide margins, three cm, say, and perhaps four cm at the top of the first page, with pages numbered, preferably in the top right corner. The first page is generally not numbered. Type 'more' or 'mf' at the foot of pages other than the last and finish your copy with the word 'end' and the wordage.

There is no rule about how the number of words should be displayed. It is usual to quote to the nearest ten if under 100 and in 50s from 100 upwards. So 76 would be 80, 564 would be 550 and 2,563 would be 2,500. It is also wise to type your name, address and phone number on the last page below your copy and the wordage.

Start the first paragraph (referred to in the jargon of the trade as 'par') – see further examples of jargon below – at the left margin but indent subsequent ones three spaces and do not leave an extra line space between paragraphs. There should be only one character space between the end of one sentence and the beginning of the next.

Give your copy a heading and if it is a long piece – several hundred words or more – break it up by inserting cross heads in the text at suitable intervals. On the whole newspapers do not like a 'frontispiece', a 'title page', call it what you will. Finally, if you're posting or delivering by hand, for two or three A4 sheets it is enough to fold them over once and use a 23 x 16 cm envelope. For more A4 sheets a larger envelope that will take them without folding is preferable. Make sure you put on enough stamps – inadequate postage does not signify efficiency. Don't forget to enclose a stamped self-addressed envelope of the same size.

Presentation of magazine features

This is more relaxed and less specific than for newspapers, but good layout with generous margins is just as important for magazines as for newspapers. Again, always use white A4 paper and double-spaced typing. Paragraphs can be indented and it is quite acceptable to leave triple spacing between them. Usually a frontispiece is included with title of piece and name of writer set out in the centre. At right hand bottom side put address, telephone and fax; bottom left hand should have number of words and date.

Payment

Once the freelance has delivered the material as specified the person who commissioned it is legally bound to fulfil their side of the contract. Payment should be made in full within a month of the delivery of the material. The exception to immediate payment in full is where the fee depends in part on the amount published, for instance, if an article is longer than was commissioned – in which case the basic fee should be paid immediately and the remainder on publication. When commissions cover a long period of time, freelances should negotiate an advance towards the total fee.

When you're starting out some editors will be generous, others less so; some will take into account research time and the fact that three live interviews are more time-consuming than one; others will give mileage; still others allowance for telephone calls. But with your first feature it's very much a case that beggars can't be choosers. Remember you're getting published; you're starting your portfolio.

Payment for published work is made without fail on specific days by the national dailies, evenings and Sundays. The Independent Group, comprising the *Irish Independent*, *Sunday Independent* and *Evening Herald*, pay weekly, but by the time payments are processed, it can take between four to six weeks from date of publication. *The Irish Times* pays within six weeks of publication. *The Sunday Business Post* pays within thirty days of the article appearing; *Sunday Tribune* contributors' accounts are paid on the last Friday of each month; The Press Group (*Irish Press*, *Evening Press* and *Sunday Press*) and *Sunday World* pay on the twentieth of each month.

Local, freesheets and smaller papers, often understaffed and with smaller budgets, are more haphazard and less willing to specify when contributors' accounts are paid.

A regular contributor to one local paper has been waiting six months to be paid for a commissioned interview she carried out for the paper. In between, it must be said, she has been paid for other work. The excuses offered by the editor have been: 'It has been posted'; 'Are you sure you weren't paid for that?'; and 'The wife washed the shirt and I had your cheque in the pocket'. When dropping in copy on several occasions and she suggested picking up the cheque, she was told variously, 'I can't lay my hands on my cheque book'; 'The least we can do is deliver it to you in person'; 'With the way you're behaving anyone would think you didn't trust us!'

If you have queries on payment, check them out with the contributors' payment section of accounts, rather than bothering your features editor.

The freelance rates of payments as laid down as basic for NUJ members will not make you rich but the good news is that they are negotiable. Most editors are reasonable and eminently approachable. Some freelances are willing to accept the minimum rate, but others who make their case coherently and factually will receive a more realistic fee for the job.

We have heard stories about ludicrous levels of payment. A freelance starting out approached his local weekly paper. A celebrity who was due to appear in their town the following week was performing in the next county. He wondered if the paper was interested in a profile. It was. Money wasn't discussed. But the editor requested 1,200 words, photographs if possible, and a deadline three days later.

The freelance achieved all three objectives. To do so he borrowed the family car, travelled sixty-two miles, paid for the coffee and sandwiches while carrying out the interview and polished his piece to professional perfection. The article was duly published and well received. He got no byline, received a payment of £20 and was asked to come up with more ideas. When he queried future arrangements about byline, payment and expenses, the editorial attitude was, 'Like it or leave it.'

NUJ rates for Irish newspapers range from £16 to approximately £70 per 1,000 words. Remember that these rates are regarded as a minimum and editors are generally open to negotiation on fees, depending on the amount of research, level of expenses or degree of expertise of the writer.

National papers

Belfast Newsletter
45–56 Boucher Crescent, Belfast BT12 6QY. Tel: (0232) 680000, fax: (0232) 664412.

Belfast Telegraph
124–144 Royal Avenue, Belfast BT1 1EB. Tel: (0232) 321242, fax (0232) 242287.

Cork Examiner Publications
Academy Street, Cork. Tel: (021) 272722, fax: (021) 275112
(*Cork Examiner, Weekender, Cork Evening Echo*)

Independent Newspapers
90 Middle Abbey Street, Dublin 1. Tel: (01) 873 1666, fax: (01) 873 1787.
(*Irish Independent, Sunday Independent, Evening Herald*)

Irish Farmers' Journal
Irish Farm Centre, Naas Road, Dublin 12. Tel: (01) 450 1166, fax: (01) 452 0876.

Irish News
113-117 Donegall Street, Belfast BT1 2GE. Tel: (0232) 322226, fax: (0232) 231282.

Irish Press Newspapers
Burgh Quay, Dublin 2. Tel: (01) 671 3333, fax: (01) 677 4148.
(*Irish Press, Evening Press, Sunday Press*)

The Irish Times
13 D'Olier Street, Dublin 2. Tel: (01) 679 2022, fax: (01) 679 3910.

The *Star*
Star House, 62A Terenure Road East, Dublin 6. Tel: (01) 490 1228, fax: (01) 490 7425.

Sunday Business Post
27 Merchants Quay, Dublin 8. Tel: (01) 679 9777, fax: (01) 679 6498.

Sunday Tribune
15 Lower Baggot Street, Dublin 2. Tel: (01) 661 5555, fax: (01) 661 4656

Sunday World
18 Rathfarnham Road, Dublin 6. Tel: (01) 490 1980, fax: (01)
490 2177

Provincial papers

Below is a list of provincial newspapers, all members of the
Provincial Newspapers Association of Ireland (PNAI). Some
will consider professionally researched and executed articles
which fit their overall strategy; others are interested in pieces
by people living locally; a few rely exclusively on staff for
features. The professional way of approaching these outlets
is to make a preliminary phone call after familiarising
yourself with at least three issues of the paper.

The Anglo-Celt, Cavan. Tel: (049) 31100, fax: (049) 32280.
The Argus, Dundalk. Tel: (042) 34632, fax: (042) 31643.
The Clare Champion, Ennis. Tel: (065) 28105, fax: (065)
20374.
The Connacht Sentinel, Galway. Tel: Tel: (091) 67251, fax:
(091) 67970.
The Connacht Tribune, Galway. Tel: (091) 67251, fax: (091)
67970.
The Connaught Telegraph, Castlebar. Tel: (094) 21711, fax:
(094) 24007.
The Derry Journal, Derry. Tel: (0504) 265442, fax: (0504)
262048. Also Letterkenny. Tel: (074) 26240, fax: (074) 26329.
The Derry People and Donegal News, Letterkenny. Tel: (074)
21014, fax: (074) 22881.

The Donegal Democrat, Ballyshannon. Tel: (072) 51201, fax: (072) 51945.

The Donegal People's Press, Letterkenny. Tel: (074) 21842, fax: (074) 24787.

The Drogheda Independent, Drogheda. Tel: (041) 38658, fax: (041) 34271.

The Dundalk Democrat, Dundalk. Tel: (042) 34058, fax: (042) 31399.

The Kerryman, Tralee. Tel: (066) 21666, fax: (066) 28011.

The Kilkenny People, Kilkenny. Tel: (056) 21015, fax: (056) 21414.

The Leinster Express, Portlaoise. Tel: (0502) 21666, fax: (0502) 20491.

The Leinster Leader, Naas. Tel: (045) 97302, fax: (045) 97647.

The Limerick Chronicle, Limerick. Tel: (061) 315233, fax: (061) 314804.

The Limerick Leader, Limerick. Tel: (061) 315233, fax: (061) 31404.

The Mayo News, Westport. Tel: (098) 25311, fax: (098) 26108.

The Meath Chronicle, Navan. Tel: (046) 21442, fax: (046) 22565.

The Midland Tribune, Birr. *Tel:* (0509) 20003, fax: (0509) 20588.

The Munster Express, Waterford. Tel: (051) 72141, fax: (051) 73452.

The Nationalist Newspaper, Clonmel. Tel: (052) 22211, fax: (052) 25248.

The Nationalist & Leinster Times, Carlow. Tel: (0503) 31731, fax: (0503) 31442.

The Nenagh Guardian, Nenagh. Tel: (067) 31214, fax: (067) 33401.

The Northern Standard, Monaghan. Tel: (047) 81867, fax: (047) 84070.

The *People* Newspaper Group, Wexford, (*Wexford People*, *Enniscorthy Guardian*, New Ross). Tel: (053) 22155, fax: (053) 23801.

The Standard, Bray People. Tel: (053) 22155, fax: (053) 23801.

The Roscommon Champion, Roscommon. Tel: (0903) 25051, fax: (0903) 25053.

The Roscommon Herald, Boyle. Tel: (079) 62004, fax: (079) 62926.

The Sligo Champion, Sligo. Tel: (071) 69222, fax: (071) 69040.

The Southern Star, Skibbereen. Tel: (028) 21200, fax: (028) 21071.

The Tipperary Star, Thurles. Tel: (0504) 21122, fax: (0504) 21110.

The Tuam Herald, Tuam. Tel: (093) 24183, fax: (093) 24478.

The Waterford News & Star, Waterford. Tel: (051) 75566, fax: (051) 55281.

The Western People, Ballina. Tel: 096-21188, fax: (096) 70208.

The Westmeath Examiner, Mullingar. Tel: (044) 48426, fax: (044) 40640.

The Westmeath & Offaly Independent, Athlone. Tel: (0902) 72003. fax: (0902) 72003.

The Wicklow People, Arklow. Tel: (0402) 32130, fax: (0402) 39309. Wicklow: Tel: (0404) 67198, fax: (0404) 69937.

Check on papers not in this listing in your local telephone book or commercial directory.

Rates of pay on the provincial papers vary from £15 to £50 per feature of 700 to 1,000 words. Some are more open than others to freelance contributions. A phone call to the editor will establish which is your best bet.

Jargon

Below are some of the most common journalistic terms:

Banner	the main headline across the top of the page
Black	a photocopy or carbon copy
Bold	thick dark type used for emphasis
Byline	a writer's name at the head or end of a story
Caps	capital letters
Caption	explanatory text, usually sited below a picture
Catchline	identifying phrase/word at top of page
Copy	any matter to be set in type
Crosshead	a sub-heading, often in bold type
Deadline	the time and date by which a story must be filed
Draft	unfinished story
Embargo	the time for publication of a pre-released story
File	to submit copy for publication
Freebie	remember there's no such thing!
Intro	opening paragraph
Lift	to pass off someone else's work as your own
Lower case	small letters
Par	a paragraph
Point	standard unit of type size, also a full-stop
Slush	unsolicited and often unwanted copy
Spike	used as a verb, meaning to reject copy
Story	article, feature, piece

4 Magazine Features

Irish writers – the ones that think.

Brendan Behan

While much of what we've said about writing features for newspaper applies to magazines, a magazine can be an easier outlet in which to make your writing début. Magazines are gentler, less frantic but no less professional in their approach and demands than newspapers. For the determined and innovative newcomer, there can be more scope there for features, columns and fillers. Again it must be stressed how all the various kinds of writing from newspaper and magazine features to short stories, novels, non-fiction, and radio pieces are surprisingly connected. This is well illustrated by Niall MacMonagle's take-off into the media, when he co-presented with Nuala O'Faolain the RTE programme *Booklines*.

Niall MacMonagle

For Niall MacMonagle, teacher of English at Wesley College, Dublin, a handwritten feature on poet Julie O'Callaghan he submitted to *In Dublin* in 1984 was his jump-off into a series of successful and varied extra-curricular activities. Having read Julie O'Callaghan's *Edible Anecdotes*, he invited her to talk to his students. While he had her captive he did the interview, which he says he took back and resubmitted in typescript. For this he subsequently received £35. It wasn't his first money. While still a student a letter he wrote to RTE earned him £5.

'I came in off the side of the street. You don't have to know the ropes to succeed in this business. But you have to begin yesterday if you want to be a writer. There's no point in saying you're going to be. You do it now.' He was first published at the age of twelve in his school magazine. 'You get a kick from seeing your name in print – it feeds into your vanity – and if you can do it once, you know you can do it again.' And again he did, being published in the *Sunday Tribune*, *The Irish Times*, *Social & Personal*, local papers in Kerry, reviewing for the *Irish University Review* and CLAI. While acting features editor for *Stet*, he was responsible for writing some fourteen 2,500 word profiles. Currently this national literary and arts newspaper is in cold storage, but phoenix-like, courtesy of Arts Council funding, it is on the point of rising again. Niall also put together features for Radio 4's *Kaleidoscope*, for RTE's *Arts Show*; and, of course, *Booklines*. His interviewees include actresses Fiona Shaw and Niamh Cusack, poet Sara Berkeley, artist Barrie Cooke. His approach to interviewing is gentle, yet firm and always prepared. 'You've got to respect your interviewees' wishes. It's too tacky and too rude to put into copy things they don't want mentioned. People are pleased when you've done serious research on them,' he says. Yet when marketing himself it's a different story. 'You've got to be assertive; go

out and knock on doors. Maeve Binchy says you need the
hide of an elephant. You can't take rejections personally. It's
so annoying when copy isn't even acknowledged and yet
when they want it they're all over you.'

There are more than a hundred magazine titles published
in Ireland and the majority regularly use freelance
contributions. The magazines range from modest budget
publications to expensive glossies. Topics covered by magazines include business, motoring – four titles; sport – sailing,
golf, basketball, greyhounds, walking; travel/tourism;
weddings – three titles; women's interest – ten titles; also
literary, Irish interest and culture, medical, historical,
religious, pastoral and theatre.

   The majority of the magazines are trade. Because these
fill a particular market niche and have a guaranteed circulation – many being subscription only – the revenue from
advertising is generous. The advertising agencies know the
publication is reaching their clients' target market. Such
periodicals can be a relatively lucrative outlet for the
freelance. When you're analysing a magazine, or indeed any
publication, never underestimate the power of advertising.
Without advertising there would be no magazines, no
newspapers, no yearbooks. The ratio of advertising to
editorial varies from 40 per cent to 60 per cent. A full-colour
page advertisement in a run-of-the-mill publication can cost
upwards of £2,000 and monochrome £500 plus.

   Areas covered by currently published trade magazines
include, in alphabetical order, accounting, advertising and
marketing, agriculture, farming and the dairy industry,

architecture, construction and property, audio-visual, the bakery trade, business management and finance, catering, computers, defence and garda forces, dentistry, education, electrical, engineering and electronics, exports, fishing, food, the grocery trade, hardware, legal, the meat trade, medical, pharmaceutical and nursing, the Irish motor industry, printing, sciences, security, textiles, transport, travel/tourism, veterinary, wine and spirit trade. In the UK and Northern Ireland, there are an estimated 9,000 periodicals, the majority using freelance contributions. It is perhaps easier for beginners to cut their writing teeth on the lower end of the local home market where, although payment can be modest, competition is not as fierce and often you'll meet dedicated editors only too delighted to pass on the benefit of their experience.

Market analysis

Market study is just as important for magazines as for newspapers. A constant beef from editors is that the vast majority of unsolicited manuscripts that land on their desk are totally unsuitable, often in all three areas of length, style and choice of subject. Even a brief analysis of the publication in question prevents this. Professional freelance magazine contributors do not make such errors. They know the value of detailed research and have too much respect for both their own and editors' time to waste it on unsuitable submissions.

You need to fine-tooth comb at least three recent copies of your target publication. Have a look at the circulation figures. Obviously magazines with higher ratings will be disposed to pay more than ones with a small readership. Be aware of the readership and know something about it. This can best be assessed from the advertising. Is its target the upmarket A1 socio-economic group or a less affluent grouping? If the cars/sports equipment advertised are top of the range or the perfume/clothes of international designer status, then you can bet that the magazine's average reader won't be booking budget holidays or looking to stretch economical cuts of meat to feed a family of seven. Also look at the ratio of editorial to advertising, and 'advitorial' (paid-for advertising material written to pass as editorial).

But your primary aim will be the analysis of the features. Are they predominantly written by staff? Have a look at the contents page – staff are usually listed. Could you write similar material? Use a notebook, make notes, get ideas as you move through the magazine. Although some pieces are written from personal experience, increasingly magazine, like newspaper features, require accurate research and/or interviewing. While familiarity of subject is a help, a professional writer can research and write on any subject with authority. Monthly magazines plan feature pieces four to six months in advance. And weekly magazines are 'put to bed' about seven weeks before they're in the bookshops. One of the pluses of magazine features is that they are generally longer then newspaper pieces. This doesn't mean that every word doesn't count nor that the articles need not be as meticulously written. In fact, it calls for even more detailed structuring; writing and personal style should be modified to suit the publication. One of the reasons for good pieces falling by the wayside is that writers put together a competent piece and then peddle it hopefully around a variety markets. Your article should always be written specifically for the particular market you have in mind.

Query letter

When you're a rank beginner, it's best first to write a query letter to the editor, briefly stating – *briefly* being the operative word – your proposal. If you've already had work published, enclose Xeroxes – up to three pieces. These will establish your credentials and give the editor some idea of your competence and writing style. When you're established and known to a particular editor, a telephone call with facts at your fingertips usually suffices. A query letter is a letter from you to an editor and you should write it as well and as fluently as you speak. Be informative, interesting and realistically honest. To sell an idea, your query letter must intelligently answer the questions an editor is likely to have. These apply uniformly to queries for profiles, issue-orientated and service pieces:

- Why is the proposed subject unique?
- Why should our magazine report it at this time?
- What is your special vantage point?
- What qualifies you as the best writer for the story?

Your query letter is a sales pitch, but it should not overinterpret your material or make promises your feature is not going to keep, as such 'hype' can lead to quick rejection of the manuscript. Nor should it be flat and encyclopedia-sounding. Here are some commandments to keep in mind with regard to making a query to a magazine:

- Do enough preliminary research to enable you to write your query with a sense of authority, setting out the slant and the most important facts of your feature.
- Address your query specifically to the appropriate editor.
- Arrange, in order of your preference, several magazines as possible markets for your idea. Always have backup markets and accept that there will probably be rejections before your idea finds a home.
- Be stylish. Your query is an indicator of your writing abilities. Write tightly. A good query is seldom more than a single-spaced A4 page.
- Arouse the interest of an editor with a few highlights, but don't tell your whole story. Save saturation points for the feature.
- Suggest the length of the piece, bearing in mind the usual lengths of pieces in the target magazine.
- Describe illustrations/photos/graphic ideas you have.
- If you have special qualifications for doing this assignment, detail them.
- Make sure to include your phone number and enclose a stamped addressed envelope.
- If you hear nothing within six weeks, follow up with a polite enquiry.
- A refusal is not a final judgement on the merits of your idea or your talents as a writer.
- Persevere in trying to sell a feature you believe in.

One accepted piece on an editor's desk is worth more than a hundred in your desk drawer.

Non-linear flow

Before starting the actual writing, focus on the spine of your piece, taking into account the magazine you're aiming for. Traditionally this was done by making a list prioritising the points. But this method can constrict freeflowing thinking and the interrelating of the various points. It is now realised that what's termed 'non-linear flow of thought patterns' achieves the best results. Remember the technique we mentioned in the section on interviewing in Chapter 1? All you do is write the main subject in the centre of the page. Radiating out from that draw the secondaries and from them the more minor relevant pointers until all aspects are covered. Try it. It's easier, more efficient and more prod-uctive than making the list.

Structure

Your opening paragraph is the one that grasps the attention of the readers and makes them want to continue with the second and third paragraphs, the next page and right to the end. Your opening should make an impact. It could perhaps be a quotation, a line of dialogue, a startling fact. But remember that while a gripping opening is vital, the remainder of your piece must fulfil the promise of the opening. Facts must progress logically from one step to the next. A good ending ties up loose ends positively. One of the professional ways is what's called 'bracketing', that is linking the beginning with the end. When you're writing, keep the format of your target magazine in mind and think in terms of layout, photography and illustrations. Make these suggestions to the editor when submitting your piece. Remember it's *your* feature and you know it better than anyone else. You have conceived, given birth and now aim to present it in the best manner possible.

Magazine success

For Rosemary it was being published in her local freesheet that gave her the courage and the impetus to try for what she calls the 'big time'. As the mother of two small children, she became increasingly interested when corporal punishment became a media *cause célèbre* and realised that this could be her break.

She spent hours, days, weeks researching and talking to the pro- and anti- lobby and compiling case histories. There was no reason why one of the national papers should not bite but that is what happened. Rosemary now views the exercise as a positive learning experience – one in which she made contacts and got herself known. She found each of the features editor she spoke to helpful and encouraging. Two weren't interested in the subject; one asked for a written proposal; one of the Sundays followed up by asking for sight, that is that she type up her piece and submit, which she did, keeping to the wordage and presenting in a thoroughly professional manner.

Despite being opposed to any form of corporal punishment herself, her piece was factual, unemotional – the sign of a true professional. Within three days the features editor rang back and said they wouldn't be picking up their option. Again she was encouraging, interested in discussing further ideas.

Feeling rejected, without even re-reading, Rosemary ran off the piece as it was and sent it unsolicited to a woman's magazine. When she rang in a fortnight later she was told that they were interested in the subject, but that this piece was more a newspaper feature than a magazine one. Which it was! It had been written expressly for that purpose. No, they weren't interested in her rewriting.

Thoroughly deflated and knowing she had broken one of the cardinal rules of professional journalism, that copy must be specifically tailor-made to suit its market, she had a second look at it, analysed the current issue of another Irish magazine and decided, yes, that her piece rewritten in magazine format could be suitable. She rang the editor, who was interested and told her the focus and the way she would like the feature presented, which required some more interviews. Three months later all 2,500 words were published.

Fillers

Many publications buy filler items, which can be thought-provoking quotations, short verse or catchy sayings. Or they can be short non-fiction pieces of 100 to 750 words. A practical short feature of this type is a single idea, tightly written, telling the reader how to:

- save time
- increase business
- do something more easily
- improve personality
- improve human relations

Get the trend? Your ideas can come from your own experience as a gardener, potholer, management expert, enthusiastic cook, wife/husband, father/ mother, DIYer – the range is great. The biggest markets for fillers are sports, hobby and home-orientated publications. Other fillers are written for entertainment or inspiration. They often consist of historical anecdotes, general interest items on unique people, business and community programmes or humour. Many magazines buy jokes. The religious press are the ideal starting marketplace for the inspirational filler. From there, you'll find many other outlets. When submitting fillers, regardless of length, type double-spaced on A4 sized paper.

It is worth while actually buying the magazines that interest you. You can analyse in more detail and will have to hand the address, telephone number, name of the editor. Check also the current edition of the *Writers' & Artists' Yearbook.*

Editors' requirements

Set out below are the requirements of some magazine editors, and just a few of the titles that welcome innovative, professionally presented freelance ideas:

Building Services News, 5-7 Main Street, Blackrock, County Dublin. Tel: (01) 288 5001, fax: 288 6966.

Electrical Review and *Futura* magazine, Unit 9, Sandyford Office Park, Dublin 18. Tel: (01) 295 8119, fax: (01) 295 8065. Pat Lehane edits these three publications; *Futura* is the trade magazine of Ireland's fashion industry. He is interested in specialist, well researched, well written and well presented freelance contributions. 'It's important that writers should analyse our journals and write in house style. A lot of unsolicited material is too general,' he says. A highly accessible editor, he favours writers who marry personal enthusiasm with professionalism, likes the telephone approach and 'people who put themselves forward'.

Business & Finance, 50 Fitzwilliam Square, Dublin 2. Tel: (01) 676 4587/676 0869, fax: 676 1978. This magazine has been published since 1964 and has a current circulation of 11,500. Editor Dan White likes the telephone approach and prefers dealing with writers who have a track record. Most financial pieces are covered in-house. He uses freelances mainly for regional copy or small business stories. 'It's vital to know the magazine. The problem with newcomers is that if they perform badly while researching or interviewing, it reflects on the magazine.' He will often request draft articles and press clippings from unknown writers.

Image, 22 Crofton Road, Dun Laoghaire, County Dublin. Tel: (01) 280 8415, fax: (01) 280 8309. A women's magazine, glossy in quality of presentation, photography, production and features. It has been published since 1974. Editor Jane McDonnell says: 'Don't ring in with your proposal. Put it in writing. Include published samples of work. Know the magazine. Check your spelling.'

Ireland's Own, North Main Street, Wexford. Tel: (053) 22155, fax: (053) 23801. Since its foundation in 1902, it has been the policy of *Ireland's Own*, a weekly magazine, to discover, encourage and foster new writing talent. Editor Margaret Galvin welcomes completed features on spec. They should range between 750 and 1,000 words in length and be informative, with a strong Irish background. Articles must be double-spaced on A4 paper and accompanied by an SAE. If you telephone or drop a note, you'll get a list of detailed requirements, as well as a copy of the current issue of the magazine.

Ireland of the Welcomes, Bord Fáilte, Baggot Street Bridge, Dublin 2. Tel: (01) 676 8871, fax: (01) 764 7656. Editor: Dr Peter Harbison. The primary purpose of this bi-monthly tourist magazine is to highlight various aspects of Irish culture. It was established in 1952, has a circulation of 100,000, mainly by subscription – 95 per cent in the US, the remainder in Britain and Australia, with a limited number on Irish bookstands. Contents include profiles, historical features, articles on houses and tourist events. An initial letter outlining an idea is favoured. If it appeals, an article of from 1,200-1,500 words will be requested, with no commitment on either side. The writer's suggestions on possible illustrations or photography are appreciated. The decision whether or not to publish will be taken immediately.

IT Magazine, 126 Lr Baggot Street, Dublin 2. Tel: (01) 660 8264, fax: (01) 661 9757. 'We are incredibly receptive to ideas. Irish magazines have a limited staff and blank pages to fill, so they depend heavily on freelance contributions, says *IT* editor, Morag Prunty. 'We're interested in specialists and regional writers to cover local happenings of national interest. But we're not enamoured of people offering us suggestions for topics we've already covered. Anybody who wants to write for us must know our magazine.' *IT* goes for ideas that have been pitched specifically at the magazine and there is little point in sending in a completed piece which, even if brilliant, probably wouldn't be read, much less considered seriously. The editor favours a written broad outline of the proposed story – bearing in mind that monthly magazines work several months ahead – and likes to see clippings of published work. If the would-be contributor has not yet been published and if an idea meets with editorial approval, he or she must be prepared to write up without a firm commission. Work, time and research are reflected by the payment received.

Jemma Publications, 51 Glasthule Road, Sandycove, County Dublin. Tel: (01) 280 0000, fax: 280 1818. *Hotel and Catering Review* and *Irish Printer* are both edited by Frank Corr. Other trade titles published by Jemma Publications are *Management*, the organ of IMI, edited by Frank Dillon; *Irish Hardware*; *Licensing World*; *Bakery World*. Frank Corr, who is delighted to be approached by freelances, favours an initial phone call and usually arranges to meet prospective writers.

'When features arrive unsolicited in the post, unless they're riveting, it's all too easy to send them back.' Even though the magazines published by Jemma are specialist, if a writer comes up with a good story or a relevant profile, lack of technical know-how need not be an impediment. If such background is required, they'll be briefed. Frank Corr is particularly interested in nationwide writers, saying: 'There are too many freelance journalists in Dublin and not enough in the regions.' Feature pieces rarely run beyond 1,000 words, and news items are 500 words maximum. 'The shorter and more tightly written, the better for me,' he says. Jemma favours copy on disk.

U Magazine, 126 Lr Baggot Street, Dublin 2. Tel: 01-660 8264, fax: 01-661 9757. Editor Maura O'Kiely says, 'It saves time and grief to make a make preliminary phone call rather than send in a feature on spec, though we sometimes find that people use up their enthusiasm on selling their idea and have little left when they come to researching and writing.' Newcomers are not commissioned, but their work is assessed, and, if not suitable for publication in the format in which it was presented, it is returned with constructive comments. 'It takes a while to get to know an editor and her idiosyncrasies,' says Maura. Openings for features in *U* include 'good interviews, hard-hitting, well-written and in-depth reports handled from several angles. People try to do features too quickly, without talking to enough different sources. Opinion pieces are not required and as for humour – too many people think they can write it!'

Woman's Way, 126 Lower Baggot Street, Dublin 2. Tel: (01) 660 8264, fax: (01) 661 9757. Established in 1963 and with a weekly circulation in excess of 60,000, this is Ireland's biggest-selling women's magazine, with a readership from the teens to the 70s, core readership from ages 25 to 40 and increasing male appeal. Editor Celine Naughton favours a written proposal, followed up by a telephone call. 'We're not a specialist publication and aim to have something for everyone. But we do focus on the human interest angle, rather than covering issues in an academic way; we tell someone's story and present it well.' She says she won't even look at handwritten copy and that if spelling, grammar or syntax are wrong, she will have little faith in the factual accuracy of the piece. She regularly receives copy with varying spellings for the same word and with incorrect names and titles of subjects.

5

Short Stories

'Discover the time of each word by the sense of passion.'

S.T. Coleridge

Sourcing a market

Short stories afford the writer an unlimited licence of creativity but the bad news is that, unless they have been written with a specific publication in mind, they require more market analysis than non-fiction. It's easier to have a passable grasp of a slant on architecture or electronic technology after studying a few issues of publications dealing with these subjects – you've only to check back copies to see if your idea has been done recently – than it is to find the right destination for a short story.

Would-be, say, science fiction short story writers should read as many of the popular magazines as they can get their hands on. They should also familiarise themselves with books by past authors and the latest hot authors. It is the only way to discover what is new ground and what is as old as the stars; what will bring an editorial shout of joy and a cheque, and what will bring through your letter box a crisp note, 'That idea was done twenty years ago.' Even beyond that, editors and successful writers agree that to write great stories, it is necessary to read great stories and to develop a wide knowledge of contemporary literature.

Despite the workload and the limited markets in major magazines, short stories are well worth tackling, if only for the discipline they impose. There are no set patterns for the creative and the innovative; the plotless short story or the prose poem may be just as acceptable as the plotted novella. Submit your manuscript, not queries, to as many publications as possible. Making sure, as we keep stressing, that your proposed outlet is suitable. If you can say you have published a few short stories, your manuscripts are more likely to be read and given consideration. Editors scout large and small magazines for new talent in short fiction, which may ultimately lead to the sale of that novel in your drawer.

The beginner is advised to check the literary and little magazine markets, which often encourage the fledgling writer and even offer personal criticism. The fee can be negligible, but these magazines offer opportunities for specialised subjects, interests and styles.

Another jumping-off point for the would-be short story writer will be competitions, and in Ireland the number of competitions has been on the increase over the past years. More about outlets further on.

Hugo Hamilton

Hugo Hamilton's newspaper experience – finding innovative ideas, research, structure and precision of writing – proved the perfect foundation for his short stories and subsequent novels.

His writing career began in the *Irish Press*, where he specialised in features. Eventually the lure of fiction could no longer be resisted and his short stories were published in the *Sunday Tribune*'s 'New Irish Writing' and *The Irish Times*. 'But the most importatnt outlet for me was *First Fiction*, a Faber anthology that comes out every few years, says Hugo. 'That gave me recognition and then Faber published my first novel.' From his current position as a novelist, he views features and his early short stories as the jumping-off points for his novels.

He describes his novels, *Surrogate City* and *The Last Shot* as 'human stories in contemporary Germany against an international background of political intrigue.' His third novel, *The Love Test*, set in Berlin, is due out in January 1995. 'While I see the strength of my books lying in research, they're also strong on plot and characterisation, frequently located in a political or historical landscape.' He completes his research before starting to write. 'You don't really know what you need until you begin writing. I thought I had too much but I used everything I had. My research was specific – Prague, Berlin, former Czechoslovakia – getting the feel of places, meeting people, asking questions. You can't get the flavour of anywhere without talking to people.'

His *modus operandi* for writing varies. He works mostly on a word processor, although he does make some longhand notes. 'I don't set any targets or limits. I just work flat out.' What tips would be give to would-be writers? 'Reading is probably the most important springboard for writers. Then, once you start writing, to get perspective, you've to walk away from your work both physically and mentally. It's often when I'm actually walking that my ideas crystallise.' Borrowing a remark from American writer Grace Paley, he says, 'I feel strongly that life is too short and fiction is too long. Tell your story and then edit and prune it. There's no point in being precious about your own work, you have to be ruthless.'

Getting started

The subtlety of the best of modern short stories depends on conveying information by suggestion. While the short story is a particularly demanding, precise and disciplined genre, its construction and compilation from the germ of an idea to polished perfection is most exciting and reward- ing. That's not even taking into account publication and the ultimate achievement – the cheque in the post.

Those lucky few teeming with ideas and characters and plot and locations all jostling with each other for ascendancy should just write. Get it all down while the inspiration is flowing. At this stage don't worry about spelling, punctuation or construction – use and enjoy the flow of the creative juices. Try not to stop, short of the house going on fire. If you interrupt this flow the momentum can be difficult to recapture. When you've finished the first draft, rest it for a few days, then look at it from an editing point of view. It is a rare short story, or indeed any other form of writing, which does not need a certain amount of editing.

If the creative juices aren't flowing refer to your notebook, discussed in Chapter 1, cross-fertilise comments, ideas;

check magazines, newspapers; allow your thoughts to roam free; try stream of consciousness. You will write. At some stage all writers suffer from block, even perhaps dislike of their work. Professionals write their way round a block by writing right through it. Hang in, keep writing, do page after page – even though you know it's going to be consigned to the wastepaper basket or edited drastically. Get something down, and the rewriting that must follow will come easier. Many writers who struggle with that raw first draft find the rewriting process fun in comparison – for here relentless spadework is replaced by streamlining for style and read-ability. Your mind has been purged by the early rush of words; now you cope with the constraints of something like a 3,000-word limit.

Mary Beckett

For as long as Belfast-born Mary Beckett can remember she wanted to be a short story writer. She has succeeded admirably with skilfully crafted, deceptively simple literary stories and a novel, *Give Them Stones*. 'When I've about two-thirds of a short story written, I think what utter and awful rubbish, but I persist and finish. For about ten minutes, I think it's not so bad. Then I decide it's terrible and I send it off in that frame of mind. When I see my stories in print, I'm usually pleasantly surprised and when I get the cheque, that's nice, though I never made much money from writing.'

While her début was with radio, she is best known in Ireland today for her published work. When she was twenty-three she entered and won a short story competition on BBC radio with 'The Excursion'. 'It stood the test of time and people still remember it,' she says. Her prize was £50 and the then producer encouraged her to submit more short stories, which she successfully did.

She then began writing stories for what she describes as small magazines. Some were published, some rejected, but she kept writing and submitting. Another lucky break occurred when she sent a story about Teresa, a Belfast woman, to *The Bell*. Its impact on then editor Peadar O'Donnell brought him north to visit her. 'He told me I was wonderful'. Mary had about eight further stories published in The Bell, and several in *Irish Writing* and *Envoy*. She first wrote a story for Radio Éireann, as it was then called, for which the fee was £4, in the early 1950s.

Her writing career came to an abrupt halt for twenty years after she married in 1956 and moved to Dublin. 'At the time I didn't feel capable of writing about Dublin and I felt I was too far removed from Belfast,' she says. 'Also I'd five children and while I was pregnant, all I seemed to be able to do was sleep. Then the family had to be reared and during those years I just didn't write.'

In the 1970s Sean McMahon and David Marcus lured her from 'retirement' to prepare a collection of her short stories for publication by Poolbeg. Around that time whe wrote 'A Belfast Woman' for the *Irish Press*, and this became the title of her anthology. Along with 'A Farm of Land', which she says nobody ever mentions, it is her favourite story. Mary's advice to today's would-be short story writers is to submit to the BBC NI, making sure the stories are the exact length;

and to competitions. In her opinion, RTE 1's Francis MacManus
Award should have its prize money reduced and be refocus-
ed on beginners. She considers that there is no alternative
but to acquire an agent if you want to be published in the
UK. 'If one agent doesn't like your work, get another. The
same applies to editors – writing so much depends on
individual taste.'

Constructing a story

A story often starts with a kernel of fact, which becomes
cloaked in inspiration and is then fused to technique and
linked into imagination. Technique is a mixture of plot and
style. A plot comprises the three Cs – character, conflict and
circumstances. Style is the way the words are used. Imagination can be described as a compound of enthusiasm,
observation, invention and sympathy.

While it's a good idea to write a synopsis and have even
an idea of the ending before starting to write, it's equally
important to be flexible. Often as the characters emerge and
come to life they determine the different conflicts. A wise
writer will give them a certain amount of freedom but never
allow them to dominate.

Somerset Maugham maintained, 'An anecdote is the basis
of fiction'. A short story, like an anecdote, must have a point
and is positively enhanced by fantasy. A short story is not a
description or a character sketch. While both decription and
characterisation are an integral part, there must be a conflict,
with crises increasing in intensity as the story progresses.

Reader or listener suspense should be maintained by the skilful moulding of the story, following the main idea step by step. This is primarily achieved by the unfolding of the characters and the introduction of fresh, but still feasible difficulties as action moves swiftly forward to the last scene, where the peak of interest is reached in the climax. The climax is ideally a surprise, but should be in keeping with what has gone before.

If you are interested in writing short stories, it is well worth having a look at some of those in *The Picador Book of Contemporary Irish Fiction*, edited by Dermot Bolger, published in 1993 by Pan Books, London.

The titles of short stories should be arresting, interesting and appropriate. The opening should make immediate and intimate contact, a keynote striking out grasping the reader/listener by the throat, demanding continuation. The best of today's short stories dive into the narrative without explanation, preamble or elaborate introduction. More than a century ago Chekov said that many a story benefits from tearing up the first half. This is even more apt for the 1990s. This is much to do with the times we live in – the technological age with its instant, bullet-point communication, the immediacy of TV, the popularity of tabloid style where information comes bare and condensed.

Telling by suggestion or implication is one of the most important characteristics of today's short story. This means that instead of spelling out in detail, you let your reader guess or know or conclude by implication. The technical advantage of this is obvious – explicit telling takes many words – and by definition a short story is short, so there is not the space to go into every nuance. But even more important, implication dilates the mind and titillates the imagination in a way that specifics never do.

The short story is decidedly end-orientated – in that we begin it with the expectation of soon reaching the conclusion. Short stories are usually read in one sitting and readers expect to be drawn along by the magnetic power of the anticipated conclusion.

Short stories have been good to so many writers, including Lilian Roberts Finlay.

Lilian Roberts Finlay

For Lilian Roberts Finlay, short stories, penned under a series of exotic *nom de plumes*, helped to educate her children. She and her husband Hugh had ten, two of whom died in a meningitis epidemic. 'In the the forties, fifties and early sixties, one man's wages would not go far. The pen came out and short stories – without any sex, romantic and bland – flew in all directions. There were many little papers prepared to pay £5 for a short story.'

The outbreak of World War II had put an end to Lilian's dreams of becoming a great actress in London. Instead she got married, decided to turn her hand to writing and for ten years bombarded Ernest Blythe, then manager of the Abbey Theatre, with scripts. Finally, frustrated by failure, she requested an interview. 'It was scathing and shattering. He told me if he staged any of my plays the theatre would be closed down by the Archbishop of Dublin.' Lilian was ahead of her time in dealing with subjects like the need for birth control, sex before marriage, marital discord, divorce. She returned home, made a bonfire of her work and determined never to write again. 'I became an enthusiastic mother, making small clothes out of large clothes and learning to knit.' Until she decided that education came before pride.

Then in 1980 with the last of her children in college, Lilian won a nation-wide short story competition with 'The Adultery', which gave her the impetus and encouragement to write a novel. When *Always in my Mind* was under consideration by Collins in the UK, her husband died suddenly. There were no savings, little money. She locked up her home, took off for Philadelphia, got a job and stayed a year. Her book was published, favourably received and and Collins asked for a sequel. 'But because the bizarre experience in Philadelphia was so fresh in my mind, instead I wrote *Stella* – a mistake. By the time I had the sequel, *Forever in the Past*, Collins had been bought by Robert Maxwell, and I was with Poolbeg. I was pleased then because they published a collection of recently written short stories, *A Bona Fide Husband*.'

Lilian, who has recently acquired a Mac, has another book in the pipeline. Several of her short stories have been read on Radio Four, others have been published in women's magazines in the UK. She says, 'When a story suggests itself, I write it and file it away for a collection.'

Irish outlets

Many newcomers to short story writing envisage their work appearing in anthology or collection form. The bad news is that you usually have to be an established author before that happens. The good news for budding short story writers is that there are many and varied outlets and these are increasing in number all the time, so getting started is becoming easier and easier. A copy of the *Writers' & Artists' Yearbook*, published annually by A & C Black, London, is an invaluable addition to your bookshelf, and will inform you of short story outlets and requirements on the international market.

When placing your short story, market research is as important – and even more difficult – than for features. As well as checking for style and general content, analyse the advertisements, as they give a true picture of target market. Before giving it a final polish it is a good idea to make sure that your story has correct slant and wordage to suit the outlet of your choice. If you're in doubt make a phone call. Editors are surprisingly approachable.

Image Magazine, 22 Crofton Road, Dun Laoghaire, County Dublin. Tel: (01) 280 8415. Monthly, 2,500-3,000 words, usually commissioned and by established writers in a literary genre. Also runs an annual sponsored competition. Watch the magazine for details.

Ireland's Own, North Main Street, Wexford. Tel: (053) 22155.

Weekly. Uses three stories per issue, each of approximately 2,000 words. Stories should be written in a straightforward style with a good yarn and should reflect the magazine's ethos of having good general appeal developed through a well-explored storyline, with an Irish orientation where possible. With submission include a brief biographical note. Each month there's a special annual edition devoted to a particular theme – Christmas, New Year, spring, summer, autumn, winter, St Valentine's Day, St Patrick's Day, a romance annual and one specifically devoted to the short story.

Reality, Redemptorist Publication, Orwell Road, Dublin 6. Tel: (01) 496 1488. Short story length, 1,000 to 1,500 words.

Sunday Tribune, 15 Lower Baggot Street, Dublin 2. Tel: (01) 661 5555. 'New Irish Writing', published on the first Sunday of each month. The requirement is a story not in excess of 3,000 words written in either Irish or English. Here the emphasis is firmly on new writers and there are more than 100 entrants each month. Published pieces are eligible for the Hennessy Award, announced in November. Prizes include £1,000 for best story by unpublished writer. Previous winners include Joe O'Connor and Colum McCann, both now with favourably received books; £1,000 for the best short story by a published, but not established writer; £1,000 for the best emerging poet, either previously published or not. A New Irish Writer of the Year is chosen from the monthly winners.

U Magazine, 126 Lr Baggot Street, Dublin 2. Tel: (01) 660 8264. 2,000 words approx, general, of high standard, consideration given to both established writers and to newcomers. Short story can be dropped in favour of good features and advertising.

The 1994 *U* short story competition is sponsored by Tia Maria. Entry form in October edition.

Woman's Way, 126 Lower Baggot Street, Dublin 2. Tel: (01) 660 8264. Weekly; two stories – 800 words, love interest; 1,200 words women's general interest.

Competitions include:

- The Works, St Brendan's, Waterloo Road, Wexford. Tel: (053) 41193. Unspecific length; general subjects
- Kill Autumn Festival; unspecific length; general subjects
- Writers' Week Listowel. Information and requirements from PO Box 147, Listowel, Co Kerry. Tel: (068) 21074.

(See also p. 147 for details of awards for radio short stories and p.170 for general literary awards and prizes.)

UK markets

Again, after studying for form and style to ensure that your story conforms, try the following:

Bella, Jackie Highe, Shirley House, 25 Camden Road, London NW1 9LL. General interest magazine for women; romantic fiction up to 2,000 words.

Fly-Fishing and Fly-Tying, The Lodge, Meridian House, Bakewell Road, Orton Southgate, Peterborough PE2 6XU. As the name suggests, fishy short stories of 800–1,500 words.

Just Seventeen, EMAP Women's Group, 20 Orange street, London WC2H 7ED. Short stories up to 1,500 words aimed at girls between 12 and 18.

People's Friend, DC Thompson & Co Ltd, 80 Kingsway East, Dundee DD4 8SL. Weekly, appealing to homemaking women of all ages. Serials 60,000/70,000 words; complete stories of romantic and emotional appeal, 1,500–3,000; also stories for children.

Playdays, Two-Can Publishing, 346 Old Street, London EC1V 9NQ. Stories up to 500 words and poems 10–20 lines for children aged 2–6.

SuperBike, Link House, Dingwall Avenue, Croydon CR9 2TA. Touring stories and fiction with with high-powered motor-cycles and associated lifestyle theme.

Take a Break, 25-27 Camden Road, London NW1 9LL. Weekly lively tabloid; geared towards women; short stories up to 1,500 words.

6

Novels

And truth severe, by fairy Fiction dressed.

Thomas Gray

The joy of fiction

Can you think of a more perfect way of earning a living than spending time weaving stories around characters you invented and whose physical and psychological attributes you dictated? For instance your hero can be tall, dark and ruggedly handsome, wipth piercing blue eyes, the brain of an Einstein, a brilliant conversationalist, internationally travelled – in other words your dream man. Your heroine can have raging red hair and the passions associated with it. She can be heading up a multinational or running her own business and be keyed into world politics and economics.

The locations where you choose to spend your deskbound hours with your fictitious characters can vary from the balmy Bahamas and the sophisticated Seychelles to the lights of London. You can commandeer the pavements of Paris or the back roads of Ireland. Your characters can operate out of hi-tech skyscraper offices, make deals with international companies, control worldwide finances. They can shop in the boutiques of your imagination for the clothes of your dreams, sip beyond-the-budget wines and enjoy the most sybaritic of lifestyles – the choice is yours. Your characters exist courtesy of you.

Dream of being a novelist? Dream of writing the book that will whisk you from your dull semi to a country mansion, a town apartment and a hideaway in the Caribbean? This and the next chapter is where we see in operation much of what we've covered in previous chapters, such as research, interview techniques, plot, characterisation, structure and, last but by no means least, dedication and determination. And let's face it: you also need a certain amount of talent and lots of luck.

Here's where we interject with a note of warning. Novel writing is the most competitive area of writing and the one where, unless you hit the big time with a book that has the buying public reaching deep into its pockets, pays poorly for time and effort. A first novel that sells well in the UK usually earns its writer less than £5,000 – in Ireland it's more likely to be £1,500.

We keep hearing and reading about the handful of giants who command fees like phone numbers squared, which is why in *Writing for the Market* we're going to explore mainly the international rather than the national market for novels. There is no reason why the next international blockbuster should not emerge from Ireland!

To date American writer, John Grisham, has earned in excess of $25m from his books, of which an estimated $10m have come from selling the film rights of *The Firm*, *The Pelican Brief*, *The Client* and his latest, *The Chamber*. Only a handful of novelists in the 1990s – all of them male and none of them Irish, nor indeed British – have achieved anything like this multi-media success. Grisham is cannily merchandised as the human being behind the bestsellers. He has sold over 60 million books and as many cinema seats.

His road to success gives hope to any would-be novelist. He taught himself to construct plots from an article in *Writer's Digest* and got up at five in the mornings to write before work. His first novel, *A Time to Kill*, was turned down by scores of publishers and agents. Once published, it failed miserably, but Grisham who believed in himself and his work, soldiered on and sold a synopsis – yes, a synopsis!– of what was to be *The Firm* to Doubleday for $200,000. The rest is history and big business.

Another big earner is Barbara Taylor Bradford, author of the prophetically titled *A Woman of Substance*. Sally Beauman, thanks to a brilliant imagination and an equally brilliant agent, became a rich women from the sales of *Destiny*, her first book. Frederick Forsyth made a fortune overnight in 1971 with his first book, *The Day of the Jackal*. This is still being read and tipped by the cognoscenti to continue as a thriller classic into the next century, like Erskine Childers's *The Riddle of the Sands* (1903) or John Buchan's *The Thirty-Nine Steps* (1915).

To write a bestseller is a bit like winning the pools – it brings fame, wealth and glory. Just as people do the Lotto each week knowing that the odds against winning are astronomical, so too do novelists and would be-novelists dream of writing a winner, the beachbook of the season. Before you start this book, be warned, though we do know that wannabee writers, particularly lucre-dazzled hopefuls, seldom listen. But *Writing for the Market* is about realism and in our book money is the most realistic of yardsticks.

Only a small proportion of novelists succeed. In Ireland Booker-Prize winner Roddy Doyle has, so have Maeve Binchy, Deirdre Purcell and Patricia Scanlan. Rose Doyle is another Irish writer who has become a successful popular novelist.

Rose Doyle

Rose Doyle consciously wrote *Images* as a 'page turner'. It sold about 10,000 copies but more importantly it whetted the appetite of English publishers and currently she is under contract to Town House in Ireland and Pan Macmillan in UK. She made a conscious decision to turn from features to fiction, saying, 'It was getting more and more difficult to be paid properly for freelance work.' She wrote a radio play for RTE; then tried children's fiction, based on the adventures of her two sons. *Tarantula!* and *The Invisible Monk* were both published by Poolbeg. But she realised that it was only with a book like *Images* that she could hope to make a financial success of fiction. She set the novel in the art world, peopled it with '90s characters and used the woman-in-distress syndrome. *Kimbay*, Rose's new novel, was published in 1994.

She's philosophical about not making money overnight. 'If you set up a small business, you've to allow yourself two to three years – maybe four – to get it going and begin to pay off. You have to resign yourself to hardly any money and a lot of work.'

Before she begins writing a book she plots a synopsis,

for use as a general guideline: 'It's comforting, like having a raft when you're swimming. If you get lost in the middle, you know you can drift back.' Her first draft is accomplished by producing a set number of unpolished pages per day and the belief that you can write anywhere. 'I find the act of writing brings characters to life. By the end of the first draft they're different from what they were in the beginning. During the second draft they change again. Plot and characters grow and change all the time.' While admitting that the future looks good, she says she served a long apprenticeship and learned from the scribblings and refusals. 'People have to figure out for themselves what they're best at.' Has Rose Doyle any further ambitions? 'Yes. A really good stage play. But I'm not finished with journalism. I'm still much too insecure to give it up totally.'

The bad news

- Only a tiny percentage of novels started get completed – the importance of determination and dedication again!
- Publishers can tell at a glance whether they want to read beyond the first page.
- By page three, they'll know if they want to publish.
- Publishers almost never commission a first book on an idea, plus an outline. You're going to have to write the lot.
- Even if your book gets published you will earn little money and unless you're extraordinarily lucky, your book will vanish off the bookshop shelves within months.

The good news

- You'll never know unless you try.
- Often the novels most slated by the critics are the ones that sell best and so can be more financially rewarding than anticipated.

Recipe for blockbuster success

Is there a magic formula for writing a money-spinning block-buster? First of all you have to realise that a blockbuster is not an ordinary novel, nor is the concept new. When you think about it, it's really only a gimmicky name for highly paid popular fiction of the time. Samuel Richardson's *Clarissa*, Mrs Henry Wood's *East Lynne* and Elinor Glyn's *Three Weeks* were all blockbusters in their day. The difference between yesterday's and today's blockbusters is that today's have become a phenomenon. Long before they hit the bookstore, airport and supermarket shelves, their lucky authors are notorious for the monstrous advances received from panting publishers. The five-figure deal up-front will be just as much a selling-point as the story tucked between the oh-so attractive cover. Publishers, besides being in love with the phenomenon themselves, are acutely aware that the mega-advance is an integral part of the whole fantasy package.

So what are the ingredients? Analyse your favourites – and before you even contemplate thinking of, much less starting to write, a blockbuster, do your market research! You'll find that today's ingredients include:

- high stakes
- larger-than-life characters
- topicality
- the dramatic question
- surface morality
- multiple point of view
- exotic setting
- passion, commitment, excitement

The other factor that has to be borne in mind is that the blockbuster market is and has always been unpredictable. While there appear to be rules or trends, the minute you try to pin them down, they seem to change. For the past few years the market has been volatile and some books written and marketed according to the commercial wisdom didn't do as well as anticipated, though 'women-in-distress' is still a firm favourite; whereas other themes, not initially tipped to don the mantle of blockbuster, are surprising both publisher and author and starting a new fashion. Against the odds of the time, Patricia Scanlan's books portraying ordinary people living in Dublin took off, captured the buying public's imagination and made her a household name.

One thing for sure – the public is not getting tired of blockbusters. But, like skirt lengths, the focus of block-busters changes. For instance the glitzy, shopping and bitch-in-the-boardroom novel so popular in the 1980s has lost favour in the 1990s. Then the formula bandied around was referred to as the four 'Ls – locations, lays, lust, labels. The locations were exotic: the boardrooms seats of power, decored accordingly and decribed in detail; the lays spectacularly graphic, with the powerful career woman often the instigator and the rather wimpish man getting his 'desserts'; the lust oozing every few pages; and the labels were designer – it was an Armani jacket, Hermes scarf, Gucci shoes, Vuitton luggage that travelled without hitch from private jet to five-star hotel. The trend today seems to be moving more towards relationships and reality, what has been termed the 'Aga saga'. A Ferrari chase in the South of France is neither here nor there if book-buyers would rather read about amorous academics in the suburbs with mortgages and dysfunctional families.

If you're not thinking of the blockbuster genre, you can people your novels with fictionalised historical figures whose lives are interwoven with the powers of the times; or you can write straight spy stories where plot and construction assume more importance than characters; children's books; international thrillers; science and fantasy fiction. The possibilities are endless. Welcome to the wonderful, frightening, scary world of novel writing. One thing we can promise is that you'll never be bored.

Although American writer John Irving, whose books include *The Water-Method Man*, *The World According to Garp*, *The Hotel New Hampshire* and *A Prayer for Owen Meany*, knew he wanted to write, it was not until he met another young writer that he received encouragement. 'It was so simple,' he remembers. 'He was the first person to point out that anything I did except writing was going to be vaguely unsatisfying.' June Considine identifies with this urge to realise personal potential.

June Considine

When she was four years old June told her mother she was a robin. Her mother answered that she was daydreaming and that people couldn't ever become birds or beasts. All they could do was to imagine the experience.

'In retrospect, I realise that this linking of mind to dream images was the budding of a young writer. But I paid it no attention,' says June. 'Work, marriage and a family came first. A busy life. No time for daydreaming.' Then, she says, one night when her two young children were sleeping and her husband was out with friends, 'Suddenly, the silence of the house was filled with promise and I picked up a pen. Floodgates opened. Words scrambled free, falling over each other in their eagerness to be expressed.

'But I knew the emotional energy needed to write fiction, the immersion in character and plot, the struggle to shape a vague idea into a credible structure, was an energy I could not spare while my children were so young.'

June became a freelance journalist. At first the features she wrote were humorous, drawn from what she knew best, family and home. Then, as her confidence grew, she began to write on wider-ranging issues. Her work covered diverse topics, from social issues to business pieces and was published in national dailies, Sundays and magazines. She edited a magazine, becoming further involved in business features, learning editing skills that would prove invaluable when she turned to teenage fiction.

Her first book, *When the Luvenders Came to Merrick*

Town, is a fantasy and can best be described as a romp through the imagination. In June's' words 'a joy to write and published in 1989.' Since then she has had eleven books published. People still ask her, 'But when are you going to write a real book, an adult book?' She says she will probably write the adult book. 'Some day there will be things I need to say which cannot be told within the confines of children's literature. Or I may write a story that will bring me a long way back in time. I shall try and remember the magic of knowing what it was like to flutter inside a blaze of russet breast feathers and allow that red red robin to bob over the keyboard.'

June Considine's life is no longer sociable. 'It's isolating, often lonely and, dare I say it, sometimes quite boring. Interaction with a computer has certain limitations, especially when I am starting a new book and realise that there are a hundred more interesting jobs to be done outside my office door. Cobwebs to be swept from under the floorboards, dustbins to be scoured with a toothbrush, grains of rice to be counted. But when the grains of rice have been counted several times, I begin.'

She works her way towards the moment when the book which she has bullied into life finally acquires its own shape and momentum. 'My mind has linked to something mysterious, call it the subconscious or a creative ether in the atmosphere, but it is a force I have learned to respect. When it happens my fingers dance on the keys, my mind hums with words that fall into place with a liquid ease that makes me forget the long-drawn-out labour pains. And when I sleep at night I dream about my characters. I see them walking through fictitious locations which I have created and hear them talking to each other using my dialogue. Imagination is a mad wonderful thing, a pool that suffers an occasional drought but is always waiting for the right opportunity to renew itself.'

While there are certainly differences between writing fiction and non-fiction, many of the same problems occur in both. With fiction you can't simply do more research if you find you're falling short of the required number of words. If you try to pad out the length of a novel it will show in the finished work and you will find that publishers send it back.

For most fiction writers it helps to have the book planned out from start to finish. If you're using exotic, or indeed even ordinary locations, it pays to have been there. Even if you deviate from the plan as the characters and situations develop, you need to know what length you're aiming at, and roughly how long you want each section of the story to run for. That way you will quickly see if it is running too fast and you can stop and re-think either the plot or the format. It may be that the idea you thought would make a great novel would actually work better as a short story or a play.

Irish fiction

Sometimes with a self-consciously literary novel it can be hard to make an accurate judgement of merit. If we don't enjoy it, we're inclined to think that we don't really understand it, and yet we might be dimly aware that it is good. The test of a thriller is simple: is it thrilling? The test of a romantic novel is just as simple: does it stimulate our romanticism? Currently Irish fiction in the UK doesn't seem to need a test. It's just working and some of it, such as Colm Tóibín's, is decidedly literary.

The craze in the UK at the moment is Irish fiction, particularly by men. Perhaps Roddy Doyle started it, but whatever, Irish male writers are enjoying an unprecedented popularity. The theme of their novels is Ireland and that old faithful, the Troubles. Colm Tóibín's *The Heather Blazing* outlines recent Irish history. Eoin McNamee's, first novel, *Resurrection Man*, covers the eruption of sectarian violence in Northern Ireland of the early 1970s. Eugene McEldowney's *A Kind of Homecoming* is the story of a double murder in the countryside near Belfast – one victim Catholic, the other Protestant. Ronan Bennett's fictional themes are similar.

But even for award winning writers like Colm Tóibín, the trail to success can be a rocky one.

Colm Tóibín

Colm Tóibín's books, *The South, Walking Along the Border, Trial of the Generals, The Sign of the Cross, The Heather Blazing*, have sold in excess of 100,000 copies. *The South* made the Booker Prize long list, was shortlisted for the Whitbread first novel prize and in went on to win the *Irish Times*/Aer Lingus award. *The Heather Blazing* was shortlisted for the 1992 Guardian Fiction Prize and for the *Encore* award for the best second novel of 1992. To date it has sold in excess of 35,000 paperbacks in Ireland and the UK.

While Colm's love is fiction, his breaks came with his non-fiction. His advice to would-be writers is, 'Finish everything you start; learn patience; make and use contacts in the publishing world and get an agent if you want to be published in the UK.'

His own writing career began inauspiciously with book reviews for *In Dublin* magazine, followed by a radio column for *Hibernia*, then general features, with topics such as wrestling matches, discos, walking around Dublin all night and the Fianna Fáil Ard Fheis. Features Editorship of *In Dublin* led to the same post in *Magill* and his travels in Africa and South America resulted in a series of colourful – rather than how-to-get-there – travel pieces.

When he began working on is first novel, *The South*, he approached an agent. 'She liked what I'd sent and said she was interested in anything I had. Your relationship with an agent is never contractual – it's one of trust – not a lifelong or a legal commitment. When I sent her *The South*, she didn't consider it ready to offer to publishers, so at her suggestion, I worked it over. She wanted an outline of *Walking Along the Border* and advised me before I began the actual writing to get a publisher, so that I'd have a contract and some money.' *Walking Along the Border* was published in October 1987 and received favourable reviews. He reworked *The South*, which he says, 'was rejected by most English publishers throughout 1987 and 1988. An agent with a small first literary novel can offer it only to one publisher at a time and they tend to be lazy and slow, so it took about two months for each one to turn it down.' He says you wouldn't and they tend to be lazy and slow, so it took about two months for each one to turn it down.' He says you wouldn't want to pay attention to the remarks in letters of rejection – one publisher said if *she* writes anything else let us know.'

Colm Tóibín was asked to contribute to an anthology on Englishness being brought out by Serpent's Tail, a newly formed publishing house specialising in literary and experimental work, first novels and work in translation. The piece he wrote whetted the publisher's interest and Colm's agent sent him *The South*. 'At end of 1988, returning from Barcelona, I stopped off in London to sign a contract and I got a two-stage advance of £1,500. *The South* was published in May 1990. Meanwhile the publishing house that had *Homage to Barcelona* was going through a change in ownership, but the book was brought out in 1990 by the English division of Simon & Schuster, who in the same year also published a collection of his writing on Africa and Argentina.

'*The South*, which came out as paperback for £7.95, wasn't really reviewed in England, but because my agent had sold only British and Irish rights, in late summer it was bought by Penguin in the States. It was translated into German, French and Dutch, and Picador then bought the paperback rights from Serpent's Tail'.

During 1987 Colm had abandoned the first six chapters of *The Heather Blazing*. Riding on the crest of good fortune, he was able to sign a contract blind with Picador, 'for good money'; and Random House bought the outline for *The Sign of the Cross*, a book about travel in Catholic Europe. 'That was me set up with work for the next two to three years.'

The Heather Blazing appeared in Picador hardback in September 1992 and was published in Spain, France, Germany, Holland and Sweden. The Barcelona book came out in Germany and Italy, and in the States in Penguin edition.

In 1990 *Walking Along the Border* was remaindered for £1.99, meaning that the rights reverted to Colm. It was snapped up and brought out in paperback by Random House, who are bringing out *Sign of the Cross* in October 1994. Picador has bought a new novel blind, scheduled for publication in the autumn of 1995 or the spring of 1996, which, he says, 'leaves me free for first time to concentrate exclusively on fiction.'

7

Books – Non-Fiction

> No man but a blockhead ever wrote except for money.
>
> *Samuel Johnson*

Selling your idea

Without bursting the blockbuster bubble, it has to be said that selling non-fiction *ideas* to publishers is much easier than selling *completed* fiction. Being able to sell an idea to a publisher, or even have an idea favourably considered, is of enormous benefit. It means that you don't have to gamble months or indeed years on a book only to discover that it is unsaleable. Even better news is that non-fiction can be a great deal more profitable than fiction in the current publishing climate, both in Ireland and the UK.

If you want to write a non-fiction book, the essential thing is to have a good idea and then to develop it. It's your idea that will attract the publisher. It is the same idea that will convince people that they should at least *think* about buying the book – pick up a copy in a bookshop, scan the cover, glance at the contents, flick through the pages, even perhaps buy it. The fate of the book depends on many factors, but without a good idea it will never be born.

Publishers are less nervous about buying non-fiction

because it has a more clearly defined market niche. It is easier for them to influence the final shape of the book than it would be for fiction, and it can be created from more than one source. Even if an author does a sub-standard job, the book may often be salvaged by editing and rewriting.

Some good non-fiction starters:

* A plump rather than a thin idea. Andy McNab's *Bravo Two-Zero* is the fat true story of the an SAS patrol behind Gulf War lines in Iraq.
* Ideas that are interesting but also of value to the reader. The most successful cookbooks, as well as being attractive to the eye and interesting to browse, offer valuable information and how-tos.
* Non-fiction books, as well as being 'about' something, are good if they have a clearly defined purpose and use. For example, *Writing for the Market*.
* If possible, visualise your readership. If you can't, you will be unlikely to sell the idea to a publisher.
* Immediacy and topicality are assets: for example, 1994 books on D-Day that coincided with the fiftieth anniversary.
* Different is good. You will have a better chance of being published if your books sounds original. There are hundreds of books about dieting but Rosemary Conley came up with a winner with her focus on hips and thighs.
* Possible is essential. When a publisher reads or hears your idea he or she must believe that you can research, write and market it.

In a nutshell, it's back to finding a market niche, as with newspaper and magazine features (Chapters 2 and 4). You must also be confident of your ability of produce the book, either because you are already familiar with the subject or because you know the research routes to take.

If you want to try the non-fiction route and if an idea hasn't come up and grasped you by the throat, refusing to let go until you get moving on it, how can you generate the necessary idea?

Ask yourself:

- What knowledge do I have that I could write about?
- Would people be interested in my speciality?
- What subjects am I interested in finding out about?

The first category might cover existing work skills, a hobby or personal experience. If you're an expert on icing cakes, you could turn that area of expertise into a book that could become a bestseller – actress Jane Asher did; if you're a keen rose grower, how about a book on that? Ex-*Evening Press* features editor, Sean McCann has written several books on the subject; Treasa Brogan's *Marry with Taste* is a successful book on getting married in Ireland; if you have had a traumatic experience involving something like illness or adoption it might be therapeutic to write about it, as Finola Batts did in *For Love of Clare*. Look at how well Darina Allen's cookery books, which are linked with her television series, are selling.

With more unemployment and redundancies, more leisure time, and increased emphasis on adult education, people are actively seeking to acquire knowledge, to learn new skills. People's specialities have become marketable skills – take for instance calligraphy, yoga, personal finance. If you're the teacher, why not think of writing a book? Doubtful? Look at the popularity of the VEC's PLCs (Post-Leaving Certificate), Vocational Training Opportunities Scheme (VTOS) and Youth Reach courses, and the over-subscribed FÁS courses. Adult education is on a growth curve that is expected to continue for the foreseeable future. On the whole, people are interested in options that are achievable, tastefully packaged and palatably presented. Writing has always captured the public imagination in Ireland and it is within most people's scope. It's an attainable dream and if nothing else, as one grandmotherly student said, 'It's a change from the telly and the bingo.'

Since most of us don't carry a whole area of expertise in our heads, the majority of professionally written non-fiction books have to be researched. For instance if you are interested in buying and selling antiques but don't make a living from it, you will have to go out and talk to people in the business; if you want to write about tennis, you'll need to talk to professionals, amateurs, trainers, tournament organisers and agents.

I decided to write *Writing for the Market* because I realised there was a hunger among the people who attended my courses for the kind of information I was giving – realistic facts about marketable work, about how to go about writing it and where to sell. The same questions cropped up again and again; difficulties were experienced in the same areas. But when I came actually to write this, while I had a wealth of facts at my fingertips, I was amazed at how much research I had to do, how many people I needed to talk to, the information I had to update. I had the same experience with my first book, *Dying With Love*. That grew out of a radio documentary, which had involved so much research that I was sure I had material not just for one, but for several books. How wrong I was. For starters a documentary is completely different from a book. The momentum of a documentary is dictated by the interview subjects; whereas a book is much more personal. Whether I liked it or not – and I didn't – to write authentically and with feeling about death I had to come to terms with my own mortality.

To write any sort of piece, you've to become passionately involved. If you're writing the book only because you think there might be a market, and the subject actually bores you, you'll have an unhappy time doing the work, and it'll more than likely reflect in the finished product. Only if you are truly interested in finding out the answers will you ask the right questions, and only if you are truly excited by the information you collect will you be able to sustain the effort of writing a complete manuscript.

The first stage in writing a non-fiction book is to submit a query.

Initial query

For the novice, a brief letter is recommended. If you are an established writer known to the target publisher, a phone call if you must. But remember that book publishing does not have the immediacy of newspapers or even magazines, and a busy publisher may be irritated rather than interested if disturbed by a phone call.

Keep the letter brief, ideally no longer than two pages. A good idea leaps at an publisher even from a short note. The second rule about the query is to keep it informal (without being slangy), friendly and lively. Thirdly, give the publisher all the data necessary to make a preliminary assessment and to encourage them to take the matter further.

Ideally your query letter should:

- begin by saying who you are and why you should be considered a potential writer
- next state the basic idea of the book in the briefest form possible, ideally in one sentence
- make clear why your book is original or at least different from other books on the same subject
- target potential readers and explain why you feel they will buy this book
- provide details about the structure and character of the proposed book, for instance if you propose using interviews, photographs
- give some idea of the factual bricks and mortar that will underpin the book
- offer to send a more thorough treatment or some sample chapters without obligation on the publisher's part. This will show that you are serious and professional.

If a publisher is interested, he or she will normally ask you to provide an outline and sample chapters. In practice, sample chapters should be the first and second and, if necessary, one other chapter. In this way, the focus and direction of your work will become clear, as will your ability to research and to analyse, your knowledge of the subject and your command of the language.

When writing your outline, bear in mind:
* the length should be somewhere between six and ten double-spaced pages
* it should provide detail on research sources

The chapters and outline may convince the publisher that the project is promising and he or she will offer you a contract, or else ask you to provide further chapters. But the important thing is that the publisher is giving you a chance and willing to work with you.

Even though you may not have a firm commitment that your proposed book will be published, you should probably go ahead and do the extra writing, knowing that your idea is a sound, commercially viable one.

Books have been based on many different kinds of personal experience. Brian Keenan's *An Evil Cradling* is a soul-searching account of his life as a kidnap victim; *Some Other Rainbow* by John McCarthy and his campaigning girlfriend Jill Morrell is a recounting of the hostage years. Remember Peter Mayle's success with *A Year in Provence* and its sequel, *Toujours Provence*? However, maybe nothing that interesting, traumatic, meaningful or exciting has happened in your life. In that case you decide to create an experience to write about. One of the obvious examples is travel writing. Dervla Murphy made her name from it, it was the impetus for Colm Tóibín and became an absorbing and successful hobby for Arthur Flynn.

Arthur Flynn

Arthur Flynn has been writing since 1975. He has written non-fiction books as well as some fiction and radio plays and television scripts. His work includes *Echoes*, a series of interviews with theatrical and political Irish figures, histories of Irish films and Irish dance and recently children's books. For the past few years he has been turning his lifelong interest in history to speciality travel books that are filling a gap in the market for tourists, local people and indeed anyone interested in acquiring an immediate feel for an Irish town or village.

It started in 1985 with his *History of Bray*, followed two years later by *Famous Links with Bray*; next came *Ringsend and Her Sister Villages*. *The Book of Wicklow*, which he co-wrote, was published in 1991. This led him to the research and compilation of *The Book of Kerry*, published in 1993. The *Book of Galway* is with his publishers and *The Book of Kilkenny* is currently being researched. 'Curiosity starts me off. First I read anything already written about the county and from that there's a chain reaction,' says Arthur. For his Wicklow book he sourced material from Lord Meath and the Powerscourt family; the archives in Muckross House, Killarney and Tralee library yielded information for *The Book of Kerry* and he found the Battle of Aughrim Interpretative Centre a mine of information for the Galway project.

'I literally research from the ground up – local libraries, the clergy and schoolteachers.' He also tapes oral history interviews with elderly people, making sure to have the text confirmed. Old books, maps and Down Surveys of the area he finds invaluable and from the National Library consults old newspapers and Lawrence Collection photographs. 'The Halls, a husband and wife team, William Makepeace Thackeray, Samuel Lewis and Arthur Young travelled and wrote about Ireland during the 1800s and they're great for quotes,' says Arthur. 'You've to be careful with libel and I come across discrepancies. They have to be checked out with the most authoritative sources and a decision made.'

The tips Arthur Flynn passes on to would-be non-fiction writers include:
- Before approaching a publisher do a detailed outline. A good idea presented badly may not be accepted.
- Study your market. Have an idea of potential sales, familiarise yourself with other books on your topic, know why yours should be published and have a reasonable chance of good sales.
- Keep a journal and a note of all the people you meet.
- Write the first draft fully.
- Edit down to accessibility.
- Aim for simple language.
- If in doubt leave out, particularly if you can't confirm the material. (Your credibility is at stake.)
- List sources and bibliography.
- Acknowledge those who helped.
- Return photographs, maps and other material.
- When doing publicity use strong, interesting facts.
- Be prepared to assist the publisher in promoting sales.

Biography

There is always a market for biographies of popular or controversial people, (especially if recently deceased) and historical figures. A biography of a film star, athlete, pop singer, criminal or politician can be an enormous potential earner for both a writer and a publisher. Kitty Kelley's racy blockbuster biographies, having left clawmarks on Jacqueline Onassis, Nancy Reagan, Elizabeth Taylor and Frank Sinatra, have both earned her a vast fortune and given her an international profile, not usually associated with non-fiction.

There are two schools of thought about whether 'authorised' or 'unauthorised' is the purest form of biography. Publishers use both words as positive selling points from different angles. The authorised biography has the blessing of the subject, which suggests that the author has more information than would have been available to an unauthorised biographer. On the other hand it can seem that the subject has had a say in what can and can't be included. The book may, therefore, appear censored to some readers.

The 'unauthorised' label on biographies suggests either that the subjects did not think the writer was of sufficient importance to merit their time or that there is something in the book which they would prefer to suppress. It can also mean that a book has been put together hastily from a collection of newspaper cuttings to cash in on a sudden surge in the subject's popularity. Often the only reason high-profile people withhold their cooperation from biographers is that they are hoping to write autobiographies themselves later and do not want anyone to queer their pitch.

Whether to write 'authorised' or 'unauthorised' is the question that dogs biographers who write about present-day celebrities. It is not a question that worries Anne Chambers.

Anne Chambers

'A biographer, I feel, is a writer under oath. You must do your audience as well as your subject justice in so far as you're obliged to present warts and all, so that the reader can make up their own mind.' It was Anne Chambers's fascination with Grace O'Malley that started her writing biography. Coming from Mayo herself, she had been reared on the legends and folklore of O'Malley but because of a lack of documentation in factual history books, she began to wonder if, like Maeve of Connacht, Grace was more legend than fact. 'I determined to find out.'

At the time with an MA in History, her career was in economic research in the Central Bank, and she found the disciplines of researching historical facts similar. 'In the National Library, where I went every evening after work, a whole new world of private and public manuscripts and references were opened up – 400-year old parchment documents, dark brown in colour, spidery writing in English, Latin and Irish. Until then I didn't know a lot about the sixteenth century – it tends to get overlooked in Irish history. Grace O'Malley was the most exciting historical figure one could find.' Anne spent three years researching and eighteen months writing. 'Holidays, tennis and discos went by the board. The story of Grace O'Malley proved fact was indeed stranger than fiction.'

'I wrote her story initially for myself, but somebody who read it suggested I send it to a publisher.' The second company approached, Wolfhound Press, took it. There was general amazement that Grace O'Malley had been overlooked as a biographical subject. Since first published in 1979, *Granuaile, The Life and Times of Grace O'Malley, 1530-1603*, has been re-printed in 1983, 1986, 1988, 1991. In the region of 50,000 copies have sold in Ireland, the UK and the US. It was 'Book of the Week' on BBC World Service in August 1987, and serialised on *Woman's Hour*, BBC May 1987. *Granuaile* was launched in Westport House, home of Lord Altamont, a direct descendant of Grace O'Malley's.

This led in 1983 to the publication of her next biography, *Chieftain to Knight*, on O'Malley's son, the first Viscount of Mayo. Anne was the first to be allowed access to the 20,000 manuscripts held by the Altamont family – '...four-hundred-year-old manuscripts that were as their authors had left them.'

Then followed *As Wicked a Woman*, the biography of Eleanor, Countess of Desmond, published in 1986, reprinted 1991, shortlisted for 1987 GPA book award. Anne describes Eleanor as one of the great tragic figures of 16th-century Ireland. 'Perhaps my favourite. Her ability to survive such a range of unbelievable personal and political tragedies that have no parallels even today.' After this book was published, Anne gave up her job with the bank and took to writing full-time.

Her most recent biography is *Adorable Diva, Margaret Burke Sheridan*, published in 1989, and whose subject's brand of humour appealed to her. Research for this, which took two years, involved two trips to Italy, one to America, five to England and several around Ireland. 'Biography is an expensive branch of literature – you have to travel to research your subjects. If GPA hadn't come up with additional funding, I wouldn't have been able to finish this. There are few bursaries available to non-fiction writers, who perhaps need them most of all.'

Her first historical novel, *The Geraldine,* is set in the 16th century. 'Although a novel it is factually based and because of my grounding in research the background is researched as thoroughly as for my biographies. Old habits die hard.'

She has acquired an agent. 'I am breaking into a new genre of writing and from a business point of view you can get bogged down on contracts, etc. The more books, the more administration.'

She says that Grace O'Malley has been 'good to her.' She scripted, narrated and presented a TV documentary *The Pirate Queen* on RTE in 1983; scripted and presented the introduction to *Granuaile* at Greenwich Concert (RTE/Windmill, 1987); co-scripted the screenplay for a feature film on *Grace O'Malley, Queen of Men*; is acting consultant on a TV documentary on Grace O'Malley with TNT; is participating in the annual O'Malley rally and the design of the new Granuaile Centre in Louisburgh, County Mayo devised as the focus of a new marketing thrust for the town. She works on scripts in conjunction with UK songwriter turned scriptwriter, David Reilly. Their 1960s comedy, *The Rathdown Lottery,* set in rural Ireland, is currently under consideration by British Lion.

8

Publish or Be Damned

Publication is the Auction of the Mind of Man.

Emily Dickinson

The Irish scene

It easy enough to start a book; the hard part comes when you're half way through and the inspiration and initial momentum are beginning to flag. Then you have to overcome doubts that you will ever reach the end, much less be published. This happens even the most competent of professional writers and even those who have a publishing contract. The only way to get to the end is by small steps – one letter after the other. One Irish writer says that on the down days when he doesn't even want to put a foot outside the bed, he tortures himself by working out that to write his requisite 2,000 words, he's going to have to put up at least 12,000 characters on screen before allowing for errors, rejigging, editing. When he has wallowed in that thought for a few minutes, common sense prevails and he knows that if he doesn't get going nobody else will do his job.

The business of book publishing in Ireland is buoyant and even during the recession has continued to grow. As well as being readers, we Irish are buyers of books. Top sellers are popular fiction, followed closely by non-fiction, such as biographies, cookery, the Royals and relationship books.

Fiction published in Ireland includes literary, popular and children's. The consensus among Irish publishers is that the worldwide market for literary fiction is slack and it's difficult for writers to sell literary first novels – remember the length of time it took Colm Tóibín's agent to place *The South*?

Virtually no Irish publisher accepts fiction from an unknown author on a synopsis only. It's too much of a gamble – a publisher must know that the author can write, plot, characterise, and incorporate dialogue. The only way to be sure is to sight the whole manuscript, but once an author's book is published, things are easier with a second manuscript. What's being published currently is well plotted, homegrown popular fiction, geared to woman readers by the pens of Patricia Scanlan and Deirdre Purcell, and relative newcomers Rose Doyle and Anne Schulman.

Up to the 1970s, children's books were not published in Ireland in large numbers, but during the past ten to fifteen years there has been a huge upsurge in this area. Children's Poolbeg, Wolfhound, O'Brien and recently Aran have all successfully filled the niche. Children's publishing is now recognised as a definite and vibrant market force, tipped to continue growing. Aspiring writers should not be fooled into thinking that children's fiction is an easier version of adult novels. It's very much an individual discipline in its own right, with children being brutally honest – as only children can – in both praise and criticism. One of the few pluses is that because books are shorter (usually around 30,000-35,000 words) they can be written in less time than adult fiction.

As pointed out in Chapter 7, it's easier to get non-fiction rather than fiction published. Good non-fiction sells well and steadily, with proven titles being reissued and reissued. The majority of Irish publishers have a healthy non-fiction list.

Unlike the practice in the UK where publishers are mainly approached through agents, in Ireland direct contact can be made and the majority of publishers are surprisingly approachable. Many editors in Irish publishing houses pride themselves on making and nurturing their own discoveries. The latest figures from CLÉ – those for 1991 are the most recent available – show that 710 new titles were published. CLÉ is a trade association for general book publishers. Its aims are to promote publishing, the interests of publishers, to facilitate training, to inform publishers about such areas as copyright and libel and generally to look after the interests of the publishing industry.

Presenting your manuscript

The house style of most publishers in Ireland is similar, but if you're being commissioned or are putting the final touches to your manuscript/disk publishers do appreciate their authors checking out with them the finer points of presentation. It makes for a more efficient working relationship between publisher and author and can save a lot of time. (See the Appendix, where punctuation and grammatical points are covered in more detail.)

Manuscripts

These should be presented in double-space typing on white A4 paper with generous margins top, bottom and sides. At the end of each paragraph use a carriage return. Do not indent by using the space-bar. If you wish to indent use a single tab position. It's not necessary to leave an extra space between paragraphs or to ensure that all paragraphs end with the page. Pages should be numbered consecutively. Do not restart numbering with every chapter.

Abbreviations and acronymns

These should not be punctuated, e.g. Mr Pat Murphy worked for the WHO before he joined RTE. Exceptions are e.g.; p. (pp.); etc.

Capital letters

Capital letters should be used for proper names and titles, (Lord Carrington, the Bishop of Meath) and for registered trade marks like Coca Cola. Convention normally decrees that they should be used for terms connected with religion, e.g. Mass, Confession. Cases where they should not be used are gardai, civil service, spring, north but Northern Ireland and the North, referring to the state. Never type headings or any word in all capitals. Use initial capitals only. Try to be consistent in your usage and consult a dictionary for guidance. If in doubt consult a good writer's dictionary – the *Oxford Writers' Dictionary* or *Hart's Rules for Compositors and Readers* (Oxford) – for guidance. But as they tend to give contradictory advice, choose one and stick to it.

Commas

These, too, should be kept to a minimum. They are not necessary in such cases as: When he returned home the cat was dead. They should be used to clarify sense and where they replace parentheses, e.g. Jane, who was just sixteen, had been given a watch.

Endings

'...ise' in such words as 'realise' and 'criticise' is on the whole preferred to '...ize'.

Hyphens

These should be unspaced, e.g. brown-eyed girl.

Initials of people's names

These should be punctuated and spaced: P. J. Donnelly lives in Maynooth. Note too that Mc, Mac and O' should not be followed by a space: P. J. O'Connor.

Italics

These should be used for emphasis, for titles of books, newspapers and periodicals, plays, films, television programmes, operas, paintings, ships, long poems – that effectively constitute a book e.g. *Paradise Lost*, for botanical and other biological names and for words and phrases in a non-English language that still seem foreign – this includes Irish. Titles of shorter works, such as poems, essays, articles and short stories should be given in single quotation marks: 'Ode to a Nightingale,' 'The Poteen Maker'.

Lists and captions

These do not require punctuation except where they form a complete sentence.

Long ('en') dashes

These should be spaced, e.g. Irish footballers – Paul McGrath and Andy Townsend

Numbers

Numbers up to ten should be written as words; numbers

eleven to a hundred may be written as words or figures, but be consistent; numbers over 100 should be written in figures. Ordinal numerals should be written as words e.g. fortieth, twenty-first. Note especially: the nineteenth century and Browning the nineteenth-century poet.

Possessives

The possessive 's should be used even with words ending in 's', e.g. Francis MacManus's novels. Sometimes euphony requires that it be omitted: Moses' tablets; Xerxes' fleet

Quotation marks

These should be single with double marks used inside single, e.g., 'John said, "I will", when I asked him,' said Mary.

Depending on the sense, quotation marks may go inside or outside full stops, commas or other quotation marks. In dialogue, the comma is put inside the quotation marks: 'How are you?' he asked. 'Not well,' she replied. In sentences that contain titles, quoted material or parts of sentences the position of the punctuation will depend on the individual case.

Spacing

Use only one space after *all* punctuation marks.

Submitting your manuscript

Ring your designated publisher, after checking that they are publishing your genre of book, and ask how they want it. We've detailed below the requirements of some publishers. One of the cardinal rules is that you always include at least a stamped addressed envelope – a stamped jiffy bag is better.

Ask when you can expect a decision – realistically it usually takes around three months.

If you submit an unsolicited manuscript, you have no right to expect any comments – good, bad or indifferent. If your work is rejected there is no point getting into an angry exchange with the publishers and writing abusive letters.

If your manuscript is accepted, you will get a phone call or a letter or be summoned to meet the publisher. Ask as many questions as occur to you. It's important to develop a good relationship with your publisher, and especially your editor. Ideally you should work together as a team to produce the best possible book. Contractually you, the author, have few legal rights. But most publishers and editors are as human as you and are only too pleased to be informed and to keep you informed. The more you and your editor liaise and the more contact you have, the better your book will be.

The publishing contract

If you've never seen a contract before it behoves you to get advice before signing. The Irish Writers' Union, 19 Parnell Square, Dublin 1, tel: (01) 872 1302 is a mine of helpful information.

The contracts being offered to new writers by the main Irish publishing houses are similar and there is no point in complaining about getting only 10 per cent royalties – it's only 7.5 per cent if you're published in paperback, as the majority of novels now are. They're the current rates and quite honestly you can either like it or lump it. The majority of writers are much more eager to get their books published than are publishers to publish them.

In a nutshell, the signing for an author of a contract means:

- You agree to deliver to the publishers your book – nowadays usually one hard copy and one on disk – on an agreed date, with contents, format and style as discussed.
- It's up to you to get copyright clearance, to organise photos, maps, diagrams, and if necessary to bear the cost.
- You guarantee your publishers that there is nothing libellous in the book and contract to indemnify them against libel actions.
- If your publishers want an index, you have to provide it at your own expense.
- You get to look at the cover, if time permits. Theoretically, you've no say in quality of paper, printing, design, binding, jacket blurb, promotion and advertising. But in practice the majority of publishers cooperate with authors.
- It's up to you to read, check, correct and sign the proofs within time specified by publisher.
- Exploitation of rights, e.g. first serial rights, translation rights, is normally controlled by publisher.
- You're expected to assist in promoting your book.

Contracts have to cover the risks taken by the publisher and there's not much, the (first time) author, can do. But one area you should clarify before signing your contract is publication date, which can be as far as eighteen months away. In Ireland where the majority of the houses have relatively small lists, publishers can delay publication of your book for business reasons if they acquire another book they perceive as having more buying appeal.

The copy editor

Publishers normally employ a copy editor. 'Editing a complicated book is rather like using a curry comb on a dog. The more high the style – romantic, heated, literary – the greater the prevalence of metaphor, the more teasing out of meaning may be required,' says Derry-based Sean McMahon, freelance editor and reviewer.

The role of a copy editor is to mediate between author and publisher. Copy editors are concerned with factual correctness, the practicalities of grammar, spelling and punctuation. The reference books they use are likely to include *Hart's Rules* and *The Oxford Writers' Dictionary*, both published by Oxford University Press. It is also the editor's responsibility to ensure that house style is applied to manuscripts.

Editors usually have a literary background, backed by acquired experience and general knowledge. 'I've a good quiz memory for trivia and will know it was Cary Grant and not Rock Hudson who starred in a particular movie; that the phrase "you're joking me" was popularised only in the 1980s,' says Sean McMahon.

He describes himself as having acquired a certain number of the requisite skills for his current work from much reading and writing. He reviews fiction and biography for the *Irish Independent* and wonders if a copy editor is a writer *manqué* who might have been an author if life had been different. In general a good copy editor will be thoroughly acquainted with modern usage (and usages of earlier ages), have a good sense of style and period, a wide experience of literature and an eagle eye for all kind of inaccuracies.

Payment

Sometimes, but not usually on a first book published in Ireland, you'll get a small advance on your royalties. Remember the telephone-number-sounding figures we bandied about in Chapter 6. Aim for them. Fine. But if you've achieved them, you should be writing, not reading this book! For the majority of us they're not realistic. More in keeping with the current publishing climate would be an advance of £500 to £1,500. Royalty payments are usually made once a year and it is your right, if you wish, to examine and query detailed statements.

Listing of Irish publishers

Below are some of the main Irish publishers, all members of the Irish Book Publishers' Association, CLÉ. Consult the current edition of *The Writers' & Artists' Yearbook* for details of international publishers.

• Appletree Press, 19 Alfred Street, Belfast BT2 8DL. Tel: (0232) 243074, fax: (0232) 246756.
Publishing interests focus mainly on non-fiction of Irish

interest, illustrated gift books as well as cookery books, promoting subject rather than author. Other areas include academic, biography, educational, guidebooks, history, literary criticism, music, photographic, social studies, sport, travel. Appletree, which has been established for twenty years, annually publishes twenty to thirty new titles. 'The first book we ever published is still in print and 90 per cent of our titles are also in print,' says publisher John Murphy. He advises new writers to approach with a publishing idea, a detailed outline, rather than an unsolicited completed manuscript. More than half Appletree's list is non-Irish, with writers draw from as far afield as Brazil. 'Because of the nature of our publishing, print runs vary from 750 to 20,000/30,000, and we publish in several languages,' says John Murphy, 'and we plan to continue for the immediate future much as we have in past.'

- Attic Press, 4 Upper Mount Street, Dublin 2. Tel: (01) 661 6128, fax: (01) 661 6176.

This press specialises in books by and about women in the areas of social and political comment, fiction, women's studies, humour, reference guides and handbooks. Attic's publishing list is evenly divided between fiction and non-fiction and it claims success with its Bright Sparks teenage fiction, with writers such as Bernadette Leach who wrote *Vanessa, I'm a Vegetarian* and *Summer without Mum.* Joan O'Neill's *The Daisy Chain War*, won the 1990 Irish Readers Association award. Máirín Johnston's *The Pony Express* took a Bisto Merit Award in 1994. Adult fiction, which sells well in the States and UK, includes *Feminist Fairy Tales*, a selection of short stories from writers such as Maeve Binchy,

Ivy Bannister, Mary Dorcey; and *Glenallen*, Mary Ryan's blockbuster. Adult non-fiction has a strong political and women's studies slant, for example, *The Women Who Won* by Una Claffey and *Irish Women's Studies Reader* edited by Ailbhe Smyth. An area where sales has doubled over the past two years is health and lifestyle, with titles such as Yvonne Ward's *Hooked? Young People; Drugs and Alcohol.*

Attic favours a preliminary phone call and if interested will request a synopsis and three to four sample chapters. Ideally final manuscript should be on disk. Decision to publish is usually given within six to twelve weeks.

Recently, Attic Press launched a new imprint called Basement Press which publishes books by men and more general interest books and also has a gay list.

• Blackstaff Press 3 Galway Park, Dundonald BT16 OAN. Tel: (0232) 487161, fax: (0232) 489552.

Blackstaff Press, established in 1971, currently specialises in publishing anthologies both of poetry and prose; biography and memoirs; cookery books; educational; fiction; fine limited editions; history and politics; humorous; natural history; photographic and poetry. From January 1994 to January 1995 some twenty-five titles, including reissues, will be published. Print runs vary from 1,000 to 5,000. This year a novel by David Rice marks the press's first excursion into popular fiction. Other titles include: *A History of Ulster* by Jonathan Bardon, reprinted three times since publication in 1992; John Waters's *Jiving at the Crossroads*; the poetry of Paul Durcan and *Clare* by John MacKenna. A covering letter, synopsis of proposed book and a few sample chapters are preferred to the submission of a whole manuscript. While receipt of copy is acknowledged within two weeks, a final decision with regard to publication can take up to six months.

- Brandon Book Publishers, Cooleen, Dingle, Co Kerry. Tel: (066) 51463, fax: (066) 51234.

Brandon, which was established in 1972, publishes biography, literature, politics, fiction, travel (Ireland), history and children's books. The focus is currently on good quality fiction, biography and children's books. Annually Brandon receives up to 400 manuscripts, all of which, editor Peter Malone assures, are assessed. 'The standard of work is generally fairly good, neither improving nor disimproving; but we have noticed that presentation has got better over the past few years.' Brandon publish Alice Taylor, Ulick O'Connor and first-time writers, and recently published a collection of Gerry Adams's short stories. The company favours a detailed synopsis of whole work, a few sample chapters, plus biographical background. Completed manuscript on disk is preferred, though hard copy is also acceptable. In 1993 fifteen new titles were published, plus several reprints.

- Gill and Macmillan, Goldenbridge, Inchicore, Dublin 8. Tel: (01) 453 1005, fax: (01) 454 9813

This firm has been established in its present form for twenty-six years, publishing annually on average eighty-five titles. A non-fiction publishing house, it specialises in secondary school books, third level publishing (mostly for post-leaving cert courses) academic publishing, cookery books by Darina Allen and Jenny Bristow; memoir, biography and some general publishing.

- The Mercier Press, PO Box 5, 5 French Church Street, Cork.
  tel: (021) 275040, fax: (021) 274969. Dublin office at 16
  Hume Street. Tel: (01) 661 5299, fax: (01) 661 8583.

Established in 1944, Mercier is the oldest independent Irish
publishing house. Initially its publishing backbone was
theology, which Vatican II rendered obsolete. Concentration
then switched to, and has remained with, Irish interest, such
as literature, folklore, history, politics, humour, ballads,
education, still a little theology and some health and cookery.
Its flagship is *The Course of Irish History,* edited by F X Martin
and T W Moody (published in collaboration with RTE) and
regarded as the bible of popular Irish History. Fiction titles have
included work by John B. Keane, and Danny Morrison. It
publishes up to fifty titles annually, including reprints.

In 1994 Mercier introduced the Martello imprint under
the editorship of Jo O'Donoghue. Her aim is the promotion
of innovative literary and mass-market fiction and non-
fiction primarily with an urban slant; and to discover and
foster fiction for young readers. She favours the submission
of complete manuscripts. Martello Books is at 16 Hume
Street, Dublin 2. Tel: (01) 661 5299, fax: (01) 661 8583.

- O'Brien Press 20 Victoria Road, Rathgar, Dublin 6. Tel:
  (01) 492 3333, fax: (01) 492 2777

This press publishes fiction, non-fiction and children's
books, in 1993 twenty-five new titles and twenty reissues.
Included in the adult non-fiction list are *A Thorn in the Side*
by Fr Pat Buckley; Feargal Quinn's *Crowning the Customer.*
Adult fiction includes *When Love Comes to Town* by Tom
Lennon, a story of gay love, and *Lottery* by Michael Scott,
who writes adults and children's horror, adventure and

folklore for Irish, English and American publishers.

Children's authors include award-winning Marita Conlon-McKenna (*Under the Hawthorn Tree* and *Wildflower Girl*), Don Conroy and Siobhán Parkinson.

O'Brien Press recommends checking their catalogue before submitting material, favours a synopsis with a section or the whole of the actual text, so that shape of book and writing can be judged, rather than a phone call, considered 'time-consuming'. Its policy is to return work that is not considered suitable within two weeks. A publishing decision can take up to two or three months. 'We like to meet authors before deciding finally how they're going to be in terms of publicity. If you write a book you're putting your name out there and you have to do publicity,' says Mary Webb, who handles publicity. 'We're in a personal business and we like to know how an author perceives his career, where this particular book fits in. We have a long-term view about taking a personal interest in our authors and we consider it important to get on well.' Depending on theme, it's O'Brien policy to have launches, 'Some books don't need them, but they're necessary for political and autobiographical books,' says Mary Webb. 'A launch is the start of getting people interested.'

• Poolbeg Press, 123 Baldoyle Industrial Estate, Baldoyle, Dublin 13. Tel: (01) 832 1477, fax: (01) 832 1430

Poolbeg, which was established in 1976, published fifty new titles in 1993. The focus is on fiction, public and women's interest, history, politics and current affairs. Children's Poolbeg, since its inception a force to be reckoned with in the promotion of writing for children, publishes the

Beachwood series, written by June Considine. Other Poolbeg writers include Bryan MacMahon (*The Master*), Patricia Scanlan, (*City Girl, City Woman*); Anne Schulman (*Intrigue*); Maeve Binchy, (*Dublin 4, Lilac Bus*), Anne Dunlop (*The Pineapple Tart*)and Michael McLaverty, (*Call My Brother Back*).

Regarding manuscripts for publication, publisher Philip MacDermott eschews a preliminary phone call in favour of a letter with a short proposal and description. If Poolbeg are interested in the idea, the author is called for a meeting and a decision made as soon as possible.

- Town House and Country House, Trinity House, Charleston Road, Ranelagh, Dublin 6. Tel: (01) 497 2399, fax: (01) 497 0927.

Established in 1981, Town House publishes commercial fiction, arts and antiquities as well as general reference and biography – in the region of fifteen titles per year. Recent books include *Lifelines*, letters from famous people about their favourite poems, edited by Niall MacMonagle; *Irish Painting* by Brian P. Kennedy; also *Check-Up,* a TV tie-in. Town House also publishes Deirdre Purcell and has recently acquired Rose Doyle.

'With regard to non-fiction proposals, a letter with an outline suffices, and always include an SAE,' says director Treasa Coady. 'For fiction we like a complete synopsis – a lot of newcomers to writing don't know how to finish books – and also two to three completed chapters.' She says she enjoys nurturing and working with the writers – it's all so individual. She follows her own instincts on books that she thinks will do well. 'It's company policy to link up as much as possible with outside publishers to make sure our writers are published internationally as well as nationally.'

- Wolfhound Press, 68 Mountjoy Square, Dublin 1. Tel: (01) 874 0354, fax: (01) 872 0207.

Established in 1974, Wolfhound publishes an eclectic selection of both fiction and non-fiction titles. In 1993 the company's output was thirty-one titles, including reprints. Says Siobhan Campbell, publishing manager: 'Print runs can vary from 30,000 down to 4,000.'

Wolfhound favours submission of completed fiction, or several sample chapters with a detailed synopsis. An SAE is necessary with all submissions.

Length of time before decision varies. 'Topical subjects are decided upon immediately. Others within three months – and if we haven't made a final decision, we'll be in communication,' says Siobhán Campbell. 'Everything that comes in is read and analysed. We have a panel of specialist readers, others who have worked in publishing in an editorial capacity, and we also read ourselves,' Recent fiction includes Liam O'Flaherty's *Thy Neighbour's Wife*, *Free Range*, short stories by John F. Deane, Frank Golden's *Two Women of Aganatz* and *Where the Trees Weep* by Dolores Walshe; books for teenagers: *Judith and Spider* by Michael Scott, and Mark O'Sullivan's *Melody for Nora*; and for younger readers, Margot Bossonet's *Skyscraper Ted* and *A Girl and a Dolphin* by Patrick O'Sullivan. Non-fiction titles include T*he Horse in Ireland* by Brian Smith, Brian Carthy's *Football Captains: the all-Ireland Winners*, *The Irish Currach Folk* by Richard MacCullagh.

9

Marketing – Your Product and Yourself

...the fashion of these times, where none will sweat but for promotion.

William Shakespeare (As You Like It)

On radio

In the earlier chapters we've spoken of the importance of selling your feature professionally – taken you step by step through the various stages. A further perk can be the interest a topical or controversial piece may generate. For instance many features are taken up on radio. Likely as not you, as the writer, will be called on to comment, amplify, either in studio or over the phone. This is a great opportunity to market yourself, an opportunity to be grasped and handled skilfully and professionally. If given a choice, opt for the studio rather than the phone. In the writing business a chance happening often opens the door to endless possibilities. Many professionals who make their living from writing maintain you've to market yourself as hard as your product. Being on the spot gives you a better opportunity.

Before you go on a radio show be familiar with its format. Is it news-orientated with questions aggressively worded and frequent use of words like 'accountability' and 'investigative'? Or is it more chatty? Be prepared. Know what points you want to put across and do so calmly without allowing yourself to become ruffled. You know your piece better than anyone, even better than an over-assertive interviewer. Keep what you say interesting, entertaining. For instance if a suitable incident occurred or there is an appropriate anecdote that you haven't included in your feature, mention it now. Over the next few days/weeks listen to some such discussions, analyse the difference between the way the professional and the amateur interviewees handle themselves. Interviewers are delighted with vocal guests and will usually give them rope to talk fluently and without prompting. It makes their job so much easier. One of their nightmares is to be landed with a monosyllabic guest. But there's a happy medium. Don't go overboard and rabbit on endlessly and without pause. Keep an eye on the interviewer. If there's nodding and smiling, continue, but if you get the chop signal, it's time to wrap up. Remember the primary purpose of radio is to entertain and to hold its listeners.

Book publicity

Marketing is even more important with the publication of a book. Many writers believe their job is to create their book and it is then up to the publisher to market it. They couldn't be more wrong. From the time of the blockbuster success of the 1980s when women like Shirley Conran and Jackie Collins and men like Jeffrey Archer marketed themselves as glitzily and as glamorously as their books, publishers have realised that the marketability of the author is almost as important as the actual book. Vocal and well-turned-out authors will sell books from appearances on both television and radio chat shows, by giving interesting newspaper and magazine interviews and by generally making themselves enthusiastically available.

Several Irish publishers say that one of the reasons they like to meet new authors before signing contracts is to assess both their personal marketability and their attitude towards marketing their book. One went so far as to intimate that they'd think again about taking on an author who wasn't willing to participate in promotional work.

Today it's recognised that in most cases, authors have to provide at least half of the marketing drive force to make their books successful. Despite what you may think, the majority of books only earn small amounts of money for their publishers. While their publicity people will try to get your work reviewed and to organise interviews with the media at the time of publication, within a few weeks other, newer titles will be clamouring for their attention and they won't have time left to devote exclusively to marketing yours. When this happens their outlook has to become mainly reactive, in that they respond to requests that come from the media but don't go out in search of opportunities. For the majority of books this level of marketing is not adequate to make any sort of a reasonable financial return for the writer.

Even for books that don't achieve huge sales the higher-profile the book and the more publicity it generates, the more helpful it will be for opening doors, getting new projects off the ground, gaining commissions. The by-product of all this is that book sales are promoted. Having a book under your belt gives a writer great credibility.

You're the loser if you don't work as closely as possible with your publisher's sales, marketing and PR people. Normally they will handle the bookstores, convincing the buyers that your book is worthy of being stocked. This is done by word of mouth and with an advance information blurb several months before publication date. The bookshop owner will be informed of the publicity slant, including the amount of advertising, reviews, interviews, all of which will stimulate customers to come into the shops to buy the book. Occasionally, some Irish publishers ask their 'prize' authors to go along in advance of publication and have a chat with bookstore personnel, mainly because budgets don't allow for much consumer advertising.

Compared to the launch of any other commodity worldwide where one million pounds is not considered a excessive promotional budget, books have to succeed with relatively small budgets. This is because the number of people who will buy a book is much smaller than those who will buy the latest soft drink or the newest washing powder.

It's up to you as the author to put as much time and thought as possible into ideas for promoting your book. Remember it's yours and you know it, its strengths, its proposed readership, better than anyone else. A gardening enthusiast who wrote a book on on his hobby came up with the idea of promotion through garden centres. It worked a dream. He gave short informal talks with question-and-answer sessions and sold signed copies of his book. By pointing out the increase in goodwill and till takings, he prevailed on the management to provide tea and biscuits.

The majority of publishers ask their authors to provide them with a photograph from which they'll have printed as many copies as required for promotional purposes. It's well worth spending a few bob having this done professionally. Take the photographer of your choice into your confidence and be guided by his professional expertise as to angle and whether smiling or serious. Remember your photograph can be a positive plus factor in persuading the browser to buy your book. People are fascinated by people, and you looking out welcomingly and invitingly from even the back cover of your book may be the impetus for sale.

The launch

Having a launch isn't written into a contract and there are pros and cons about it. If you have a strong marketing and PR team working at promoting your book a launch isn't as important as if you're with a do-it-yourself publisher, who feels his responsibility begins and ends with having the book published. Some publishers refuse to fund launches and of recent times in Ireland writers are doing so either out of their own pockets, by sponsorship or having the cost deducted from their royalties.

It's a good idea to have a 'personality' to launch the book officially. If they're media-worthy, this will generate photographs and editorial coverage, which will reflect on your book, yourself and ultimately your sales. Your publishers will have their own list of media people, journalists, specialists, and you'll be asked for a list of, say, twenty to fifty people you wish to invite. Don't be tempted to comb the highways and byways for lost relatives and friends you haven't seen since your schooldays. By all means include family and close friends. A launch is a nice way of saying thanks to those who have helped and been supportive during the creation of your book. But primarily use your guest list as an opportunity to further sales of your book.

Most book launches are held around 5.30 to 6.00 pm to facilitate members of the press. The usual launch format is that after about half an hour of general socialising, the publisher introduces the personality to the assembled guests, who will say a few complimentary words about your book and yourself, in the hope of making all those present want to acquire a copy. Then the publisher will speak briefly before introducing you.

At this point we're going to interject a mention as to what you should wear – how formal or informal you should be. Your choice of clothes depends a lot on subject of book, launch venue and the personality doing the launching. For instance a book about homelessness, launched in the Simon Community headquarters by the Minister for Health presents a much different situation from that of a novel with night-clubbing as its central theme, launched by an internationally acknowledged high-flier in one of Leeson Street's well known night spots.

Check in advance where you'll be sitting or standing, from where you're going to speak, and on microphone facilities, if any. Do have your spiel well prepared. Write it out in its entirety; then write pointers from the text on card(s) and rehearse in front of a mirror. While you're rehearsing, keep an eye on your body language. Are you too immobile? Waving your hands like a demented flapper? Jigging from one foot to the other? Have you a petrified expression? Unless you're used to speaking publicly, it's by practising in advance that you'll shine on the occasion. And you will. Keep what you say short, pithy and to the point. Have your written speech and cards to hand. But it's unlikely you'll need them.

The desired outcome of a launch will be interviews, perhaps a diary mention, but this may happen only if you're a big name or have written an obvious winner of a book.

Extra publicity

Marketing yourself is a demanding and thorough business. Whether or not you're having a launch, in conjunction with your publisher's marketing team you should work towards:

- Setting up radio, television, newspaper and magazine interviews. (When you're doing several interviews, it's a good idea to 'space' or 'spread' your most impact-making points, so that the same item won't be occurring over and over again. A writer of non-fiction who is an old hand at drumming up publicity makes a list of about ten of the most interesting points and 'doles' them out sparingly to interviewers.)
- Making sure bookshops have your book in stock – particularly if you're on local radio or being interviewed by the local paper. Your book should be readily available and on the day of promotion, not three days later.

- Sussing out and recommending reviewers – the majority of publishers are happy to send review copies of the book to any journalist or broadcaster who is interested. So if you have contacts, had dealings or know of anyone who'd be interested in plugging your book, give their names to your publishers. Good reviews or bad – it really doesn't matter as long as the title is correct – move a book off the shelves.

- Word-of-mouth promotion – the best way, particularly in Ireland, to popularise a book. Get that moving by convincing an influential core to read and recommend. A recommendation from the Gay Byrne, Gerry Ryan or Pat Kenny shows can result in a sell-out within twenty-four hours.

- Originating features. A feature on the subject or one of the angles of your book is an excellent way of promoting it. To get a features editor, magazine or newspaper, interested, use your original synopsis – the one you used to sell the book to the publisher. Work out which branches of the media are likely to be interested in which aspects and chose a maximum of two angles for each publication. Discuss this with your publishers before you get in touch with editors. Unknown to you they could be negotiating for serial rights and your plan could jeopardise theirs. About three months before publication write to editors of monthly and weekly magazines; a month before publication notify the national and local press. If your book is of specialist interest make sure it goes to the relevant correspondent. It's a good idea to write an advance master article, summing up the main storyline in about 1,000 words. This clarifies the key message of your book, gives you an available skeleton for instant adaptation and provides you with a piece to send to editors on a speculative basis. Not all editors consider they should pay for such pieces, believing that free publicity is reward enough. You have to weigh up the pros and cons of this, but we think it's usually worth doing, though you can't promote your book as blatantly as in an advertisement. Don't keep mentioning the name of your book in the text of the feature. The editor will either reject the article or cut out the mentions. But you should be able to work in a mention – as a footnote to the article, hopefully with publisher, price and date of publication, perhaps a reader enquiry number on the subhead introduction or on a picture caption – important, as many people who only scan magazines don't read features but do absorb pictures. However, the latter won't happen unless you include a photograph and it's unlikely to be returned.

- Thinking up different and innovative angles and outlets for publicity
- Approaching local radio stations yourself. While your publisher's marketing department will approach obvious television and radio producers, there's nothing to stop you having a go yourself considering your work from a different angle. Authors are good communicators and thoroughly familiar with their subject. They make good interview subjects and usually generate good response on phone-ins. Though that doesn't always happen. I went on an hour-long supposed phone-in on a local radio

station. Despite the despairing entreaties of the interviewer, not one call came in; so we spent the time in studio live on air swapping life stories, recalling amusing incidents, remembering anecdotes. Because of the professionalism of the interviewer and his ability to redirect and to think on his feet, it worked.

- A brief word on television appearances. The researcher usually checks what colour women propose to wear. Red, cyclamen and royal blue come across very well whereas yellow and green are not the best of screen colours. If you're only visible from waist up, avoid being too fussy with collars, earrings, brooches and keep neckline simple. If the whole of you is on display, think of the way you present in your entirety. Have a dress rehearsal and assess yourself in front of a long mirror. For men it's much simpler: the suit, shirt and tie present a clean line. You needn't worry about make-up. That's professionally and flatteringly applied to both men and women, including your hands.

- Promotional tours are not generally considered necessary for books published in Ireland. But if the subject matter of your book is suitable and is of considerable interest to the general public, you could be asked to do a promotional tour. This takes in talks, local radio newspapers and book-signings.

It's advisable to allow at least a fortnight before and a fortnight after publication for positive promotion. You need to be in good fettle. If you thought selling your book to the publisher was demanding, you don't even known the meaning of hardship until you've explored and exploited every promotional avenue.

Having a book published and promoted professionally opens all kinds of doors to talks, features, interviews, panel discussions and the next book. If your book is non-fiction, whether you like it or not, you'll generally be regarded as an expert on your subject. I remember giving a talk shortly after the publication of *Dying with Love*. In the audience was a hospital chaplain, who asked my opinion on his handling of a specific incident. He was eminently more qualified than me in the area of dying, but because I'd written a book, which I might add was drawn from case histories rather than personal experience, he regarded me as an expert.

10 Writing for Radio

Look in thy heart and write.

Sir Philip Sidney

General guidelines

For those of you interested in writing for radio, the most important fact to keep in mind is that material to be listened to has to be written differently from material to be read. With radio it's how your script sounds that is most important. The best radio writing frequently looks awful in print, with incomplete sentences, conversational words and repetitive phrases. Good radio is simple, yet sophisticated – an intimate medium of personal word pictures.

Like submissions for print, radio scripts should be typewritten, double-spaced one side of A4 white paper, with pages clearly numbered and your name, address, telephone number and a stamped addressed envelope (international reply coupon when dealing with the BBC) enclosed. Most amateur scripts fall by the wayside because they are not written expressly for the spoken word. The way to get tuned into the listened word is to listen, listen, keep listening and analyse. Regularly study the *RTE Guide* and the *Radio Times*. They give a picture of what's happening on radio, information on new programmes, seasonal changes and producers.

The outlets included in this chapter are by no means definitive. They have been chosen to give you a feeling for the requirements and variety of the market.

As we opened *Writing for the Market* with features, which are relatively short, and progressed to novels, we will take the same route with radio. It is likely to be easier to make a radio début with a short piece rather than a story, play or documentary. But don't think short mean easy. Both *Matins* and *Sunday Miscellany* pieces are cameos that illustrate what's best in radio writing. Scripts for both these programmes are read in studio by the author, who needs adequate rehearsal to achieve a professional standard of delivery, checking intonation, pacing, pauses and unusual pronunciation. Record, listen back and adjust, if necessary.

Matins

The requirement is for five sixty- to ninety-second scripts either individual or thematic, but with a spiritual theme. Submissions to John MacKenna, Editor Religious Programmes Radio, RTE Radio 1, Donnybrook, Dublin 4

Sunday Miscellany

Broadcast on RTE Radio 1 on Sunday mornings from 9.05 to 9.50. Scripts of 700 words or five minutes long may be on any topic of general interest, for example history, travel, biography, personal reminiscences, short literary pieces or poetry.

'The cardinal rule of writing for *Sunday Miscellany* is to remember that you're writing for speech,' stresses producer Lorelei Harris. 'But it's also about the author's ability to deliver on their script and the way it fits in with the overall

composition of the programme. *Sunday Miscellany* is a lot
to do with the chemistry between the different pieces.' She
receives up to a hundred scripts per week. 'As much as we'd
like to, we have neither the time nor the resources to engage
in individual analysis of proposals we reject.'

Address to Lorelei Harris, *Sunday Miscellany*, RTE Radio 1,
Donnybrook, Dublin 4.

Voice Over

This offers real opportunity and is open to newcomers who
get the chance working with professionals to interview, script
and present. It's a half-hour programme slot which can take
the form of reportage, documentary, studio discussion.
Recent topics included the Youth Parliament; Commercial
Travellers; The Growth of Golf; the Amateur Dramatic
Movement. If you've an idea that you consider suitable put
it in writing to Bill Meek, programme adviser, *Voice Over*,
RTE Radio 1, Donnybrook, Dublin 4.

Local radio

As yet local radio in Ireland has not realised its potential
with regard to broadcasting short stories, plays, talks,
documentaries – markets that, it was hoped, would emerge
for both aspiring and established writers. If you're interested
in writing for local radio, it's a decided advantage to be from
the area; and it is best to make personal contact with the
programme co-ordinator. The following radio stations are
worth noting:

• Highland Radio, Pine Hill, Letterkenny, County Donegal.

Tel: (074) 25000, fax: (074) 25344.

Contact Danny Sharkey – on his weekly show he uses short stories and poems and does interviews with authors.

- LMFM, PO box 95, Boyne Centre, Drogheda, County Louth. Tel: (041) 32949, fax: (041) 32957.

'There's a wealth of writing talent but it's not being exploited properly,' says Ciaran Kissane, LMFM programme co-ordinator. The arts programme accepts scripted fictional and non-fictional material; selected writing competitions tied in with promotions are run throughout the year. The station does consider material submitted speculatively, but as there isn't the facility to produce, tends only to accept recorded and produced work.

- Radio 3, William Street, Tullamore, County Offaly. Tel: (0506) 51333, fax: (0506) 21293.

Transmitting to counties Laois, Offaly and Westmeath, Radio 3 has a three- to six-minute short story slot. Stories, submitted on cassette if possible, should be relevant to the area, entertaining and ideally include a touch of humour.

Aspects of radio

Much of what has been covered in previous chapters also applies to writing for radio. Additional aspects that should be kept in mind include audience, theme and technique.

- Audience: Radio listening is often a solitary pastime, in the car, in the kitchen, out in the garden, in bed. If you don't hold attention it's all too easy for your audience to switch stations or turn off.

- Theme: An unadorned, unaffected theme, with a simple plot, economy of scene and character. Material laced with humour and suspense works best.
- Technique: Use plain language, simple sentences and words. Write for listening; avoid tongue-twisters; omit stage directions. And very importantly use word pictures liberally. For example from Wolsey's speech in Shakespeare's *Henry VIII*, 'the killing frost'; Dylan Thomas describes the little town Llareggyb in *Under Milk Wood* as 'bible-black'; and doesn't the sentence: 'When he laughed the room grew smaller' say all? To check that you've 'radio-speak', tape your piece and play it back. Does it sound like the spoken word? The best radio writing leaves that magical and enigmatic margin, that space of the invisible, which must be filled in by the imagination of the listener.

Short stories

Short stories for radio have many of the characteristics of the modern short story written to be read. They often start with a kernel of fact or fantasy, or even a phrase, fused to technique and linked to imagination. As we've said, compression by suggestion and implication is one of the great charms of the modern short story, particularly the short story for radio where information is best conveyed indirectly – a series of almost impressionist images works well. A good radio story lingers on the palate, leaving a powerful aftertaste. If you're short on ideas use the idea triggers we covered earlier on.

Back again to market research and analysis. If you've never written a short story for radio and are interested in doing so, it's worth investing in *Prize-Winning Radio Stories*, an anthology based on the first eight years of the annual Francis MacManus Short Story Award, edited by Michael Littleton, features editor, RTE Radio 1 and published by Mercier Press, costing £6.99. Sit down and analyse the construction, characterisation and narration of the various stories.

Francis MacManus awards

In Ireland the Francis MacManus awards is one of the main outlets for radio short stories. While entry date and number of words required are regularly broadcast, if you're entering the competition it's a good idea to get a copy of the current years rules and conditions, available on request from RTE, as details may vary from year to year. But these rules are general:

- The competition is open to people born or normally resident in Ireland.
- Stories, in English or in Irish, should be written for radio and must not have been previously published in any medium.
- Entries which must be typewritten, should be within the range of 1,850 to 1,950 words. Make sure to retain a copy as scripts aren't returned.
- The winning author will receive £1,500 and a commemorative trophy. Three additional awards will be made, one

each of £750, £500 and £250 for second, third and fourth
places respectively. In return RTE Radio has the right to
broadcast one of each of the winning entries with subsequent broadcasts, if any, attracting payment at current
rate of payment, i.e. £90.

• Other entries of high standard may also be broadcast by
RTE radio.

• Acknowledgment of entries is made only if the entrant
provides a stamped self-addressed envelope.

Entries for the competition average around 1,000 scripts.
An internal reading panel in RTE reduces the scripts to
around thirty, which are then passed to outside judges who
make a final decision under an RTE-appointed chairman.
Over the eight years the competition has been running the
judges have included Maeve Binchy, James Plunkett, Deirdre
Purcell and Eavan Boland.

Margaret Dolan

Margaret Dolan, winner of the Francis MacManus award in
1992 and 1993, says radio is her forte and that she's an
addict. 'I love listening – I'm an ear person – and it's my
favourite medium to write for.' She says if you want to write
for radio, it's important to listen to radio – a lot of it. She
favours writing in the first person, to heighten intimacy. 'The
best radio is as though you're talking to one person, and,
unlike television viewing, the majority of people listen to
radio on their own.'

Margaret's stories often begin with a floating idea, a

snatch of thought, and are rarely written in one sitting. 'For instance, the phrase 'wire me to the moon' – the stimulus for the title of the story that won last year – came to me one day as I was walking across the fields. The finished story ended up a pastiche of different ideas from way back. I find memories come and go, with bits remembered from maybe twenty years ago finding a home, slotting in with other pieces, which I weave into each other and polish until I'm satisfied. But you've to be careful not to edit the feeling and heart out.'

'Tomkis Square Park', which won her the award in 1992, is her favourite story. 'It started me off and gave me hope and encouragement, opened other doors, gave me confidence to go on. It gave me the courage to ring up Philip MacDermott of Poolbeg to ask him about publishing a collection of short stories and from that came *Nessa*, my first novel.' *Ever-Rest*, a black comedy radio play about euthanasia, was broadcast by RTE Radio 1. She is currently working on her second novel, has another radio play and a television play in the pipeline.

BBC Radio Four

BBC Radio Four broadcasts a short story five times a week at 4.45pm. Since the slot was moved from morning to afternoon, listenership has doubled. New writing is welcomed, but it has to be up to standard and to compete with published, classic and commissioned pieces. The type of story favoured varies, but the common ingredient is suitability for radio. Guidelines from the BBC state, 'Bright, upbeat entertaining tales, with a narrative-led plot which tells a good story without gratuitous sex or violence. Stories shouldn't be cluttered with too much dialogue, character, description and digression. The golden rule is economy. Tell your story clearly, unfussily and authentically.'

Stories from the regions, which for BBC purposes includes Ireland, are transmitted on Tuesdays and Thursdays. The slot length is 14'30", requiring stories between 2,300 and 2,500 words in length. A brief covering letter explaining writers' track record should be enclosed with submission. There is no need for a story synopsis, nor for a cassette recording of the text. Stories with a regional bias of interest should be sent to the nearest BBC Regional Centre, which for both Southern and Northern Ireland is Belfast. Address manuscripts to Short Story, BBC NI, 25/27 Ormeau Avenue, Belfast, BT2 8HQ. Otherwise send to The Short Story Office, Room 623, Broadcasting House, Portland Place, London W1A 1AA. Scripts are acknowledged within a few weeks, though final consideration usually takes a minimum of two months. If you're thinking of a topical theme, bear in mind that stories may be recorded fourteen weeks ahead of transmission.

Plays

The almost telepathic transference of images from mind to mind is the beauty and the glory of the radio play. Still one of the most celebrated pieces of radio is *Under Milk Wood*, Dylan Thomas's 'play for voices', first heard, narrated by Richard Burton, on BBC Third Programme in January 1954.

The radio play gives the writer extraordinary imaginative scope. Working on the principle that anything described can be imagined, a radio play can travel between centuries and continents. It can take place in exotic locations or within the confines of a single mind. But such freedom imposes its own limitations, requiring discipline of structure, awareness of the nuances of language and an ability to maximise the power of silence and the techniques of sound effects – all to stimulate the listener's imagination, remembering that radio audiences are held by sound alone.

Dialogue is the dominant element in a radio play – it advances the story and fleshes out the characters. While interesting, exciting dialogue carries a play a long way, other elements of sound, including silence, are used for impact and for listeners to assimilate what's happening. The art of dialogue on radio is a sophisticated form of 'shortspeak' – natural without being too explicit. But the stringing together of conversations is not radio dialogue. To achieve smooth flowing naturalness, the scenes and individual lines have to be structured with great precision. A radio play may predominantly consist of dialogue but one that's 'all talk' in a static conversational sense is the ultimate in boredom.

Alan Titley

Alan Titley's writing break came when *Tagann Godot* was produced on RTE Radio 1. The play won the Oireachtas prize for drama in 1987. 'Afterwards I didn't know what to do with it. The Abbey said they weren't interested. So I sent to to

RTE and it was done on radio.' In 1989 it won the Pater prize, awarded by Australian Academy of Arts and Scientists for international radio drama. The following year it was produced in the Peacock Theatre.

When he gets an idea there is no dithering about its ultimate shape – it immediately presents itself as a story or a play. He completes research before he starts writing and knows his direction. 'An idea may take years to come to fruition, but when it's ready it comes quickly. I don't write a sentence until I know where it's going to land.' Writing part-time he has completed plays in five weeks. 'I concentrate on getting it all down and then editing with the promptings of a producer. Producers know what works dramatically. Radio is great; you've freedom to do anything from earthquakes to the opening of the Red Sea.'

He can't remember when he first started writing but he does know that pre-TV he was always 'scribbling stories in jotters'. He was an avid reader and as a teenager a regular in the bookshops in his native Cork. At college in St Patrick's (he wanted to be a primary teacher) he'd great lecturers, particularly in English and Irish. One day while a group of them were talking about writing, one said to Alan, 'Why wouldn't you do something like that yourself?' Alan says, 'You remember encouraging remarks like that.'

After graduation he went to Africa. 'I worked hard, read voraciously, wrote stories and articles and produced plays,' says Alan. 'Then I started into my first novel, typical autobiographical rubbish, but frightening in that a fictional incident I included about being arrested actually occurred. From then on my writing has been drawn from fantasy, imagination or history – never personal fact.'

On his return to Ireland he wrote a few novels and stories in Irish, which he insists, 'are better forgotten'. Since then Alan, who admits he'd much prefer to be a creative writer than an academic, has had several radio plays on both RTE and BBC 4, including *Scissors* and *The Long Drop*. In 1986 he won the Butler prize for a collection of Irish short stories. He has written in Irish a study of the novel and is included in the Field Day Anthology. *An Fear Dána*, the story of a thirteenth-century Irish poet, was published in 1993 by An Clóchomhar, a publishing house specialising in Irish academic books.

'I've no shortage of ideas. I've hundreds, from books of history, anecdotes, things people tell me,' says Alan. 'In Ireland we've too much confessional literature. I don't see writing as as a therapy for people's neuroses. It's a craft you work on to produce a story, a novel or a play, whatever way it comes to you.'

Structuring a play

Many playwrights say that outlining a play is the hardest part, more difficult than the actual writing. No unwritten work ever wants to be outlined. But we reckon that writing a play without an outline is rather like building a house without a plan. The main problem with an outline is that we're forced to visualise a play that may not yet be completely formed in our mind. If research is incomplete, our characters lifeless, our plot unfocused, writing an outline is an almost impossible task.

The few stabs I made at doing an outline for *A Marriage of Inconvenience* had to be jettisoned until I had completed my research and indeed given it time to settle. Also the story and my lead characters had to become an integral part of me. Once that happened the outline wrote itself. An outline is not a rigid contract, rather a sort of a promise. When we write an outline, we're saying in effect, 'This is how I reckon the play will turn out, but I don't guarantee every detail'.

If you're at the idea stage you may submit to both RTE and BBC a brief outline together with some pages of dialogue. Unless your work is known, the submission of a synopsis results only in a general response. But you will have made contact and you will have ascertained that your idea is not already in the pipeline. The following is a possible procedure that may even be successful:

- Know story (research, characterisation, plot).
- Write outline.
- Know destination and length of play.
- Work out number and length of scenes: from two to five minutes approximately works well.
- For each scene separately list content, characters, location, acoustics/effects.
- Write, rest, rewrite.
- Submit.
- Keep your fingers crossed.

Below are some practical guidelines issued by RTE Radio Drama, which equally apply to a radio play for any outlet :
- Scenes should only be as long as necessary.

- When nearing end of scene, subtly prepare listener for next one.
- Avoid stage directions for producer's benefit only. If they are important to the play they should be indicated in the dialogue.
- Radio drama should stimulate, leaving the listener to supply mental images in response to what is heard.
- The only way of establishing characters' presence is to have them speak or be named. Too many in a scene confuse the listener.
- Sound effects should be regarded as useful additions, rarely as substitutes for dialogue.
- As radio involves only listening, individual scenes and the play as a whole should be constructed so as to provide a variety of sounds to hold the listener's attention. This can be achieved by

    length of scenes
    number of people speaking
    pace of dialogue
    volume of sound
    background acoustics
    location of action

- There is no formula for writing a successful radio play. It requires the basic techniques of good dramatic writing, plus an imaginative awareness of the restrictions and advantages of a medium where nothing is seen. It is only by listening that a writer can begin to judge what works and what doesn't.

Presenting your script

- Scripts should be typed double spaced on one side of A4 white paper.
- Names of the characters should be separated from their speech and typed in underlined capitals in a separate column.
- Names should be given in full throughout.
- Description of sound effects or other technical directions should be clearly differentiated from spoken parts of scripts.
- Include with play, synopsis and cast list with brief notes on characters.
- Number the pages consecutively.
- Frontispiece should include play title, your name, address, telephone number.
- It's worthwhile getting script bound.
- Keep a copy.

Sample Script

Warm-up by Kevin Grattan (p.31)

> FX: CAR PULLING INTO DRIVEWAY. DOOR
> BEING OPENED AND CLOSED.

1 <u>MOLLY</u>:   It's just what you need. You'll
enjoy it.

2 <u>BETTY</u>:   I would like a job. I've always had
an interest in nice clothes.

3 <u>MOLLY</u>:   Having an older person there will
be reassuring to the mature client
while the younger ones will
probably treat you rather like a
mother.

> FX: HALL DOOR OPENING AND CLOSING

4 <u>BETTY</u>:   I'm not sure I like the word
'mature'. Anyway, what's to lose...
we'll see!

> FX: LIVING ROOM DOOR OPENS AND DON
> COMES IN

5 <u>DON</u>:   Oh! Hello Molly.

Radio plays have to conform to a precise length. But there is no sure method of measuring this against number of words or pages. The best way is to read aloud against the clock, making allowances for effects, music and pauses.

RTE

At any one time RTE has 120 play scripts under consideration. They receive 600 per annum, 550 of which are unsolicited. Receipt of script is acknowledged within days, but decision can take many months. Each submission is considered by at least two expert readers. Current play slots include (and it should be noted that the main demand is for the shorter plays):

- *Plays Peculiar*, (30 min) – zany, innovative
- *Theatre of the Air* (45 min)– a mix, varying from adaptations to historical, biographical
- One hour slot – more for established writers. Theme, structure, atmospherics, pacing, twist, are all of vital importance
- Classic serials, 30 min.

Submissions with SAE should be sent to Laurence Foster, Editor Radio Drama, RTE, Dublin 4, Tel: (01) 643111.

The P.J. O'Connor Awards

The aim of the annual P.J. O'Connor Awards is to encourage writers of radio drama and to give the amateur drama movement an opportunity to perform on the national radio network. Announcement as to date of submission, is made in early autumn over national radio. Category A is for writers, with the winner receiving £1,000, runner up £750 and £500 to the second runner up, as well as being produced professionally. A further six plays are selected for the Amateur Drama Radio Festival with authors receiving £250 each. Writers showing promise are invited to attend writers workshops.

The rules include

- requirement: 30-minute plays in Irish or English, specifically written for radio
- writer should be Irish or resident in Ireland
- competition open to new writers and writers with a maximum of two hours professionally performed radio drama
- no correspondence entered into, no entries returned

BBC

BBC Radio Drama offers the freelance writer one of the largest and most wideranging markets in the world. They receive 250 scripts per week and at any time have 1000 under consideration. Scripts are acknowledged within days, but a decision takes several months. Outlets include:

Drama Now (up to 75 min), dedicated to new and challenging work

Studio Three (up to 45 min), exploratory and experimental use of sound

The Sunday Play stage classics and major dramatisations

The Monday Play (75 or 90 min), showcase for original writing on complex themes, classic stage plays, dramatisations of novels

Saturday Night Theatre (75 or 90 min), traditional family entertainment

The Afternoon Play (30, 45 and 60 min), largely original, with a significant number by new writers

The Classical Serial (60 min weekly episodes), a mix of dramatisations of old and new popular and major works

Sixty Minute Series (60 min weekly episodes), usually four, self-contained episodes, but with continuing central characters. Strong storyline with a bias towards detection

Thirty Minute Serials/Series (30 min weekly episodes), two to eight parts, popular appeal material, light comedy, romance, detective, hard-boiled genre thrillers

Wednesday Afternoon Series (45 min three to six parts), mostly original serials and anthologies

Festivals Radio drama regularly broadcasts festivals and seasons of plays across all slots

Feature Programmes (normally 30-45 and 55 min), broadcast on Radio Three and Radio Four with a wide range of subjects and styles. Propose subject before embarking on speculative script.

Reading – Published work is broadcast in *Book at Bedtime*; Early morning readings (cheerful episodic pieces) when parliament is in recess; *Reading Aloud*, a 30-min non-fiction slot.

Submissions from southern and northern Ireland can be sent

to BBC NI, Broadcasting House, Ormeau Avenue, Belfast BT2 8HQ or to the Literary Manager, BBC Radio Drama, Broadcasting House, London W1A 1AA.

Documentaries

While opportunity always exists for the talented amateur who can interview and compile to high standard, the majority of RTE's and BBC's general documentary slots are commissioned from people recognised as professional documentary makers. The biggest fault with newcomers, producers say, is that they expect to be able to make documentaries without ever having listened to them. Says one, 'Documentaries are a difficult way for people to start into radio. You really need a professional background.'

But opportunity does exist in RTE's religious programmes. Of the eighteen forty-two-minute documentaries that went out over the past year, there were eleven different presenters and five first-timers made their documentary débuts. There are also half-hour and fifteen-minute slots – 80 per cent of the latter's presenters being newcomers. 'The themes we look for are spiritual in the widest sense,' says John MacKenna, commissioning editor religious programmes radio. Recent documentary subjects include the story of the TB sanatorium in Wexford, Christian Brothers and mythology.

If you've a documentary clamouring to be made – and it should clamour and you should be passionate about making it – the way to set the wheels in motion is to submit a one-to-two page proposal in which you set out the focus of your documentary and list proposed interviewees and their relevance to the subject. Don't presume that people will be delighted to be interviewed. Check with them – nothing could be worse than to get agreement in principle only to find that people won't talk to you. Explain that you're carrying out preliminary research with the aim of compiling a documentary and ask if they would be interested in taking part. If they're not enthusiastic, find someone else. Also include a brief biography of yourself stating experience, if any, in terms of recording material. If your proposal is accepted, a producer will be in touch with you to discuss structure, format of interviews, costs, fee, deadline.

Julian Vignoles

'A reporter goes in the front door, while a documentary-maker uses the back door,' says Julian Vignoles, senior radio producer with RTE, winner of the 1991 and 1992 Jacob's Award for Radio Documentary with *No Meadows in Manhattan* and *Death of a Farmer.* He has made about fifteen documentaries over the past four years.

Words, sounds, music and silence are the ingredients of a documentary. 'The most important point to be realised about a radio documentary is that with sound only you've to hold an audience,' says Julian Vignoles. 'There are no hard and fast rules about making a documentary and you don't necessarily need a clearly defined story.'

Julian doesn't know where his ideas originate. 'You have to be able to see the possibilities. For instance the first time

I heard Mary Coughlan singing 'The Magdalene Laundry', I just knew there was a story behind the song and after a few phone calls, I realised I'd a powerful documentary.' It was a documentary that became a talking point and stirred public conscience – the story of girls and women who became pregnant outside marriage and were consigned to a life of seclusion, degradation and atonement. The poignancy was enhanced by inserts from Patricia Burke Brogan's award-winning play on the same theme.

Julian says that good documentaries are born from more than title and description. 'You've to develop an instinct for recognising a story that can run for forty minutes and that can't be done as well on live interview. The best document-aries have stories behind stories – of human interest, the human condition – and are told by technique. With a good documentary when you add two and two you get five, not four.'

He says he doesn't record a huge amount of material – around two and a half hours, which he listens to once for overview; then he marks off the inserts, looking for an impact-making beginning and end. 'Sound effects are important only if they're an integral part of the story but they've to be subtle, not obvious.' He cites as ludicrous an interviewee talking about waking up to the singing of birds overlaid with a sound effect of birdsong, though he does consider that a documentary benefits from an acoustic element.

His more recent documentaries have had more narrative input, using his own voice for links. On occasions he leaves in the questions. 'A documentary shouldn't be seamless; you've to create a mood. Some are better without narration, others with,' he says. 'The material collected dictates the shape and the theme, the mood and formation. You should aim for impressionism, rather than being too obvious or too literal.'

Making a documentary

When putting together a documentary, I have informal meetings with proposed interviewees, so that we can become relaxed with each other, discuss the project and talk without the pressure of recording. This facilitates compiling questionnaires, allowing linking answers to be woven, so that the documentary can be created with the minimum of narration – the format I favour.

In the case of my documentary on adoption, *Mothers and Daughter*, the original central character decided not to go ahead and I spoke to several people (wondering if the project would ever get off the ground) before coming up with what was the final combination.

The recording machines most used are the Sony Professional and Marantz. It is vital to be completely familiar with the workings of your recorder and to try it out in various circumstances, locations and with different people. If you're using a chrome tape – generally recommended – set the dial to chrome; check and if necessary adjust the recording dial with each interviewee and keep a constant watch that recording level is registering. For each interview start a new tape, number and label clearly; make sure microphone is switched on; bring spare batteries; record some 'silence' and other acoustics, if

required. The more advance planning, the more professional
the outcome.

After recording, the next step is to listen to your tapes for
an overview, decide which inserts you'll use, time them. When
the beginning is earmarked the remainder seems to fall into
place. Next comes structure and compilation. At this stage, you
should consult with the producer about music and sound.

From a marketing point of view, if your documentary is
topical or one with a human interest you'll probably be able
to do either a newspaper or magazine feature – or indeed
both, from different angles – ideally arranging for
publication around the time the documentary is transmitted.

The sample page below should clarify layout – unlike a radio
play, characters are numbered in sequence throughout a
documentary script.

Sample Script

Mothers and Daughter by Patricia O'Reilly (p. 1)

FX: Music – 15 secs. Then running under to end 1. 'at all'.

1. tape 3, 177-187
Teresa
'When I was young, I idolised Madonna'…'It didn't happen like that at all.' (27 secs)

2. tape 1, 003-037
Terri
'It was on a Friday and I was going to meet her'…'drill going inside me, I was shaking so much.' (71 secs)

3. tape 3, 012-025
Teresa
'The journey down was fine'…'to say goodbye to my parents and Margaret-Mary.' (33 secs)

4. tape 2 110-121
Mary
'When the social worker came'…'well, they must be getting on great.' (33 secs)

5. Narrator
It was an emotional occasion for all concerned. Terri was meeting her daughter for the first time in eighteen years. (12 secs)

m\f

11

Extra! Extra!

Writers seldom wish other writers well.

Saul Bellow

Agents – literary

Agents are interested in representing writers who are writing books (both fiction and non-fiction) films or plays and some short stories.

The role of an agent is to sell his clients' work. If you're positive, highly motivated and brimming with ideas on how to market your material, you can manage without an agent, particularly if you're selling in Ireland. If you want to break into the UK and international markets, an agent is necessary.

The majority of publishers have agents with whom they do business – those who have sold them books that did well and those who dealt fairly and efficiently.

Agents provide selling, negotiating and legal service. They can help you decide how to market your writing to reap the maximum benefit. Some may help to improve a writer's financial situation considerably by getting better deals and arranging subsidiary rights sales. But the initial impetus on any project must come from the writer, the instigator of the idea, the creator of the work.

Most agents have a low profile, yet they are very much in demand and can pick and choose the authors they take on. Trying to find an agent can be as soul-destroying as trying to find a publisher – at least with a publishing company you can get its list, or from bookshop-browsing get an idea of the kind of work it publishes, whereas with an agent you don't even have such a firm foundation for market analysis. What makes this stage of the hunt so depressing is that even if you do get an agent, you and he have still to find a publisher.

Many Irish writers have agents based in London; they are usually acquired by personal recommendation.

You have to sell yourself and your ideas to agents as hard as you have to editors. Don't inundate them with massive manuscripts. Start with a letter which sums up in a few paragraphs what your book or script is about. If you're selling fiction, include a few sample pages from the beginning of the book. When you've found an agent who agrees to read and comment on your work, you may be getting objective and professional advice, but don't hold your breath. Like publishers, the majority of agents work slowly. You may hear nothing for months; then you can receive a printed rejection slip, just as impersonal as from a publisher.

Agents sell what you send them. They don't act as your commissioning agent from editors and publishers. If you've a straightforward idea for a book which you can get accepted by a reputable publisher, go ahead. You'll be offered a standard contract with standard terms. In such a situation there is little an agent can do to improve on the deal you can get for yourself. There is no point in giving ten per cent of your fee to an agent. Agents can succeed in messing up a good relationship by being too aggressive with the publisher.

The best work to send an agent is that which might be legally complicated or which has the potential to sell into a number of different markets. A good agent will have international contacts in publishing and the media. He or she should have a wealth of legal experience and should be able to unwind any legal intricacies, whether national or international, dispensing with the need to employ a solicitor.

Currently there is only one agency in Ireland: Jonathan Williams Literary Agency (1981), 2 Mews, 10 Sandycove Avenue West, County Dublin. Tel and fax: (01) 280 3482. He specialises in general fiction and non-fiction, preferably by Irish authors. He suggests revisions and doesn't usually charge a reading fee.

Bursaries

The Arts Council is the statutory body which promotes and assists the arts in Ireland. It is funded by the exchequer and the national lottery and provides financial support and other services. It offers bursaries in literature to assist the development of creative writers (drama, fiction, poetry) by enabling concentration on specific writing projects in either English or Irish.

Since 1991, the Arts Council and Aer Lingus have collaborated in operating Artflight - a scheme that offers opportunities to people working in the arts to travel outside Ireland. In addition travel grant applications for up to £750 are assessed four times per year.

The Author's Royalty Scheme in conjunction with the Arts Council assists publishers through grants/loans to pay royalties to writers in advance of publication. A special provision has been made for translations of Irish to English.

Further information is available from The Arts Council at 70 Merrion Square, Dublin 2. Tel: (01) 661 1840 (1850 392 492 local call charge from anywhere in Ireland), fax: (01) 676 1302.

General awards

(Specific awards for short stories are covered in the relevant section of Chapter 5 and awards for radio writing in Chapter 10.)

The following are open to Irish-born or Irish residents:
Macaulay Fellowship
Fellowships valued £3,500 are awarded once every three years to writers under thirty years of age to help them to further their education and career. Next literature award is 1996. Further information from the Arts Council.
The Marten Toonder Award
£3,500 for literature in 1995 in recognition of established achievement. Further information from the Arts Council.
Bisto Book of the Year
An annual award, a first prize of £1,500 and three prizes of £500 each, to a writer or illustrator of children's books.

Details from Irish Children's Book Trust, Irish Writers' Centre, 19 Parnell Square, Dublin 1. Tel: 01-872 1302.

GPA Book Award

£50,000 awarded every three years for fiction, poetry or a general work (autobiography, biography, history, essays, belles-lettres and criticism). Details from Award Administrator, GPA House, Shannon, County Clare. Tel: (061) 36000.

Irish Times Literary Prizes

Drawn from nominations in English or Irish submitted by literary editors and critics. Approximately £7,500 for non-fiction, £7,500 for a first book of creative literature, £10,000 international fiction prize.

The Rooney Prize for Irish Literature

£5,000 awarded annually to encourage young Irish talent. Details from J. A Sherwin, Strathin, Templecarrig, Delgany, Co Wicklow. Tel: (01) 287 4769.

The following is a further selection of prizes and awards. While UK-based these are open to Irish entrants:

The Booker Prize

Annual prize of £20,000 for best novel published each year. Further information from Book Trust, Book House, 45 East Hill, London SW18 2QZ.

Bridgeport Arts Centre Creative Writing Competition

Annual prizes for poetry and short stories. First £1,000, second £500, third £250. Details from the competition secretary, Arts Centre, South Street, Bridport, Dorset, DT6 3NR.

Children's Book Award

Awarded annually to authors of works of fiction for children published in the UK. Further details from Jenny Blanch, 30 Senneleys Park Road, Northfield, Birmingham B31 1AL.

Arthur C. Clarke Award

Annually £1,000 for best science fiction novel first published in the UK. Titles are submitted by publishers.

The Catherine Cookson Fiction Prize

Annual award of £10,000 for an unpublished novel of at least 70,000 words written in style of Catherine Cookson. Further details Transworld Publishers Ltd, 61-63 Uxbridge Road, London W5 5SA.

Crime Writers Awards

Details from PO Box 172, Tring, Herts HP23 5LP.

Encore Award

Annual award of £7,500 for best second novel of the year. Details from The Society of Authors, 84 Drayton Gardens, London SW10 9SB. Tel: 071-373 6642.

The Ian St James Awards

£25,000 prize money for writers of ten short stories of 5,000-10,000 words and six short stories of 2,000 to 5,000 words. Further details from The New Writers' Club, PO Box 101, Tunbridge Wells, Kent, TN4 8YD.

Whitbread Literary Awards

Open to novels, first novels, children's novels, biography/autobiography, poetry. Details from The Booksellers' Association, Minister House, 272 Vauxhall Bridge Road, London SW1V.

Income tax exemption

Income tax exemptions can exist under Section 2 of the Finance Act 1969 for original and creative works having a cultural or artistic merit. Further information from the Office of the Revenue Commissioners, Secretary Taxes Branch, Blocks 8-10, Dublin Castle, Dublin 2. Tel: (01) 679 2777, fax: (01) 679 9287.

Irish Writers' Centre

The Irish Writers' Centre, 19 Parnell Square, Dublin 1. Tel: (01) 872 1302, fax: (01) 872 6282, provides both accommodation and an administrative structure for:
- The Irish Writers' Union
- The Society of Irish Playwrights
- The Irish Children's Book Trust
- The Irish Translators' Association

Other organisations at the Writers' Centre:
- The Irish Copyright Licensing and Collection Agency, director Muireann Ó Briain. Tel: (01) 872 9090.
- CLÉ (Irish Book Publishers Association), administrator Hilary Kennedy. Tel: (01) 872 9090.
- Ireland Literature Exchange concerned with the promotion of translation of Irish writing. Tel: (01) 872 7900, fax: (01) 872 7875.

The basic aims of the Centre are:
- to assist writers to pursue their work

- to promote cultural exchange of a literary nature between Ireland and other countries
- to organise and promote literary activities
- to cultivate interest both at home and abroad in the work of contemporary Irish writers

PEN

This is a world association of writers was founded in 1921 to promote friendship and understanding between writers and to defend freedom of expression within and between all nations. The initials PEN stand for Poets, Playwrights, Editors, Essayists, Novelists. Membership is open to all writers of standing who subscribe to its fundamental principles. Further details on the Irish branch from secretary Arthur Flynn, 26 Rosslyn, Killarney Road, Bray, County Wicklow.

Tyrone Guthrie Centre

The late Tyrone Guthrie's home in Annaghmakerrig, Co Monaghan is a workplace for writers, artists, sculptors and musicians supported by the both arts councils in Ireland. The main house accommodates up to eleven artists who contribute what they can afford towards the cost of their stay. There are also five self-catering apartments. Enquiries and applications should be made to Bernard Loughlin, resident director, The Tyrone Guthrie Centre, Newbliss, County Monaghan. Tel: (047) 54003, fax: (047) 54380.

Writers groups

At last count throughout Ireland there were more than a hundred writing groups. Some met weekly, others fortnightly during the winter months; still others were in contact all year around. Writing is a lonely business and the support of a group of like-minded people on the same wave length can be beneficial. But be careful. Assessment of work destined for publication is better carried out by an outside professional, rather than at group level, which is why the most vibrant groups have regular 'guest' speakers. Where can you make contact? Try local libraries and bookshops.

Appendix: Grammatical Nuts and Bolts

I will not go down to posterity talking bad grammar.

Benjamin Disraeli

There are two common attitudes to grammar: a shuddering belief that it is boring and useless and the conviction that if its complex rules can be mastered, the ability to write superb English will be assured. Neither view is correct. But what is useful is a good understanding of how sentences are constructed and a familiarity with common grammatical terms.

The three elements of writing are: words, sentences and paragraphs.

Words

Words are a writer's basic tools. Select the best to do the job, that is, to say exactly what you mean. Every word should help to create a picture in the reader's or listener's mind.

- Strive for brevity, clarity and vividness. Don't use 'contribute' when you mean 'give'.
- Simplify technical terms. 'Carcinoma' is cancer.
- Avoid unnecessary wordiness in all forms and use simple

words when possible. 'A member of the canine species' is 'a dog'. A spade is a 'spade', not 'a long-handled agricultural implement utilised for the purpose of dislodging the earth's crust!'

- Be specific. Inexactness is as bad as wordiness.

  Vague: A bunch of flowers

  Specific: A bunch of red roses

- Avoid trite phrases. They're the mark of amateur or of downright laziness. Such phrases include: 'this point in time', 'fit as a fiddle', 'in the pink of health'.

Beautiful Words

A competition run in one of the British national newspapers to find the most beautiful words in the English language came up with the following in order of popularity: melody, velvet, gossamer, crystal, autumn, peace, tranquil, twilight, murmur, caress, mellifluous, whisper. Nice, aren't they? Just beware of overusing them.

Sentences

A sentence is a group of words that expresses at least one complete thought. This means that something definite is said and for this to happen the group of words must contain or imply a finite verb. The subject of a sentence is the person or thing who (that) performs the action. The predicate is the part containing the action (not just the verb). In the sentence: 'The woman travelled to Cork,' 'The woman' is the subject and 'travelled to Cork,' the predicate.

Generally:

- Never crowd too many details into a sentence.
- Avoid repeating the same words or phrases in the same sentence or paragraph.
- For journalism, use short, snappy sentences and clear words.
- For features/fiction, while there is more leeway in these genres for greater complication of sentence construction, style and colour, still keep to the maxim of conveying exactly what you mean to say.
- For radio, again aim for precision, but edit for 'radio-speak' and look for opportunities to insert 'colour pictures.'

Paragraphs

The cardinal rule for paragraphs is that they should contain related ideas and function as a unit. Currently in journalistic news stories, particularly tabloids, paragraphs average around thirty words. There are fewer limitations for features, though generally newspapers use shorter paragraphs than magazines. Fiction is individual and dependent on style. In writing for radio, while sentences and paragraphs will not be neatly rounded off, remember that the listener's mind can grasp small units of thought more easily than large ones.

Parts of speech

Adjectives tell us more about a noun and express a characteristic, quality or attribute e.g. *rosy* apple, *red* bus, *French* bread. It has been wisely said that the adjective is the enemy of the noun. If a crisis is always 'acute' and an emergency always 'grave', what is left for these words to do by themselves? If a decision is always qualified by definite, a decision by itself becomes a poor filleted thing.

The most polished and stylish of writers use adjectives to make their meaning precise, rather than emphatic, reserving them to denote kind rather than degree. 'The proposal met with opposition and is in danger of defeat,' is more powerful than, 'The proposal met with noisy opposition and is in obvious danger of defeat.'

Beware in particular of pushy adjectives of vague intensity, such as considerable, appreciable and substantial. Try not to use these without asking yourself, 'Do I need an adjective at all?' If so would a more specific one suit better? If not which of these three words, with their different shades of meaning, serves my purpose best?

Adverbs tell us more about verbs, such as the word 'quickly' in, 'They walked quickly.' Also described as adverbs are intensifying words such as 'very'; negative participles, 'not'; and sentence connectors, like 'however'. Adverbs are often classified by the kind of meaning they express e.g. time (yesterday); place (there) and manner (slowly).

Adverbs answer in advance the questions 'How?', 'When?', 'Where?', 'To what extent?', or 'Why?' by replies, such as 'precisely', 'today', 'here', 'completely' and 'consequently'. There are also what are called adverbs of assertion, like, 'yes', 'no', 'perhaps'; and introductory adverbs: such as, 'accordingly' and 'however'.

What has been said under the heading of adjectives is

equally true of adverbs. They're best used sparingly to give precision rather than to add emphasis. Distrust ones that vaguely intensify, such as 'very', 'considerably', 'appreciably'; and those that vaguely mitigate, like 'relatively', 'comparatively', 'rather'.

Nouns are traditionally defined as, 'the name of a person, place or thing'. Nouns are generally subclassified into common, proper and collective.

- Common – as the name suggests, are the most frequently or commonly used e.g. woman, bush, hope.
- Proper – refers to a particular person or place e.g. Sandra, Kildare.
- Collective – indicates a group e.g. audience, team.

Prepositions stand before a noun to show its relationship to something else. Notice the position of 'over' and 'into' in the following sentences. 'The ball shot over the net.'; 'We went into town.' Prepositional phrases, such as 'in connection with', 'in regard to', 'in relation to', are often overworked.

One of the hallowed 'rules' of grammar is that a sentence shouldn't end with a preposition. Don't hesitate to ignore this, if your ear tells you that's where the preposition goes best. The very rule itself, if phrased, 'Do not use a preposition to end a sentence with,' has a smoother flow and a more idiomatic ring than, 'Do not use a preposition with which to end a sentence!' Churchill once said, 'It is the sort of pedantry up with which I will not put!'

Verbs are traditionally defined as 'doing' or 'action' words, displaying contrasts of tense, aspect, voice, mood, person and number. However, it is more difficult to define the meaning of verbs than the traditional definition suggests –

many such as 'be' and 'seem' are not action words at all. Verbs dictate tense, traditionally classified into past, present and future. The trend with modern writing is to use the present tense to give a sense of immediacy, of the story happening on the spot. The verb is the core of any sentence or any clause. Watch verbs. Whenever possible use active voice and the simple past tense. They inject life, action and movement into sentences.

'The tea was made by Alice.' can be a weak sentence. How much stronger is, 'Alice made the tea.'

Verbs generally occur with a subject, for example, 'She arrived', and dictate the number and nature of other elements in the predicate. Some verbs govern an object, for example, 'She saw a car.' Others govern an adverb as well: 'I put the book there.'

Punctuation

Punctuation is becoming increasingly sparse and streamlined. Unnecessary commas in the heading of letters, pages splattered with dots and dashes are to be deplored. The semi-colon is under threat and the colon rarely used except to introduce a list of items. This makes it all the more important that punctuation be used correctly. Is this passing of punctuation a matter for regret or for congratulation? Certainly much old fashioned punctuation served no purpose, as the meaning was clear anyway. But it must be said that English is much enhanced with precise punctuation.

Punctuation marks alphabetically listed:

Apostrophe (') used mainly:

- to indicate possession e.g. 'the cliff's edge'; 'the farmers' tractors'. Because the apostrophe was placed before the 's' in the first example, it shows we are writing about one cliff; it position after the s in the second phrase denotes more than one farmer.

- to signal the omission of letters or numbers e.g. 'he'll', 'the '90s'. Incorrect usage of the apostrophe is increasing both in errors of omission, when it should be present as in, 'the girls hat,' which should read, if just one girl is in question, 'the girl's hat; and in errors of addition, when it should be absent, as in, 'I saw the cat's,' which should be, 'I saw the cats'; and in wrong placing 'is'nt' being presented instead of 'isn't'.

Brackets (()) Often words or phrases, additional to the main statement, are introduced into sentences. These insertions are known as parentheses and can be set apart by using brackets, commas or dashes, like, 'The party of visiting actors (they were the director's special guests) were treated like royalty.' Brackets are also useful for explanatory words, 'We discovered his speciality was crêpes (pancakes).'

Colon (:) Opinions vary about the proper use of the colon in punctuation. It has to a large extent gone out of fashion. It mainly functions now being between two sentences in antitheses, as 'Man proposes: God disposes.' (Antitheses are thoughts or words balanced in contrast). It also introduces lists.

Comma (,) marks a short pause in the flow of a sentence. Not to be used instead of a full stos and only when really necessary. The comma is more felt than learned by rule.

'He was, apparently, willing to support you' throws a shade of doubt on his bona fides. Whereas with 'He was apparently willing to support you', 'he' becomes a more savoury character.

Dashes (–) have many legitimate uses, though not as many as ascribed by people who treat them as a labour-saving punctuation devices. They should be employed with discretion. The following are recognised usages:

- To introduce a correction, amplification or explanation of what immediately precedes it, 'The plan is concerned with the situation years ahead – say in fifteen years time.'
- To gather together the subject before completing the sentence: 'The severely crippled, the social misfit, the mentally unstable – all have been helped by the new act.'
- In pairs for parenthesis, 'Fiona Barr – the actress – read the script'. 'A memorandum – copies are enclosed for the information of the Board – has been issued to the school management committee.'

Full Stops or *Periods* (.) are punctuations marks whose main function is to signal the end of a sentence. Use plentifully. Always choose a full stop, rather than a slighter stop when what follows has no real connection with what goes before, for example, 'There are about 630 boys in the school, and the term will end on April 1.' There should be a full stop, rather than a comma, after 'school'. Other usages of the period include the markings of abbreviations, although the tendency today is increasingly to omit it.

Hyphens (-) indicate a division within a word. They may appear at the end of a line of print, where a word will not fit without a break (excla-mation), or to mark the parts of a complex word, such as a compound (father-in-law).

Quotation Marks (") also called inverted commas, signal dialogue. The traditional mode is 'Don't worry,' his friend hollered back. 'It's a small thing.' or 'Don't you have a bath at home?' she said. Single quotation marks (") have largely taken over from double ("") apart from the USA.

The *semi-colon* (;) is used to bring together two sentences closely connected in meaning, but not linked by a conjunction ('and' or 'but'). If the subjects are the same, a semi-colon is particularly appropriate. It makes a longer pause, a more definite break in the sense, than a comma. At the same time it punctuates a clause or sentence too closely related to what has gone before to be cut off by a full-stop. 'The company is doing some work on this; it may need supplementing'.

Problem areas

'Affect' or 'Effect' – A rule of thumb is that 'affect' is more commonly used as a verb and 'effect' as a noun. The usual meaning of 'affect' as a verb is 'bring about a change in' e.g. 'His behaviour affected me greatly', though the verb does have a few other uses such as 'pretend to feel,' as in, 'She affected indifference.' The usual meaning of 'effect' as a verb is 'bring about', as in, 'How shall we effect a solution?' The everyday use of 'effect' is as a noun meaning 'result' ('The effect was remarkable'), or 'influence' – to have an effect on somebody.

'Due to' and 'owing to' – the difference between them? You'll never be wrong with the following mnemonic, 'Due to means causeD by'; 'Owing to means because Of'

Gender of Pronouns – A long-standing controversy exists about the appropriate pronoun to use in sentences where such words as anyone, everybody and someone are subject: 'Anyone can do what...want/s.' The pronoun 'he' used in a generic way is traditional, but can draw criticism for its male bias, but 'she' is decidedly odd. Though not grammatically correct, 'they' is now commonly employed.

'None' – This word is one of the chief targets of purist criticism. Depending on construction, it is found with either a singular or a plural verb. When it precedes or refers back to a singular noun, the verb is also in the singular, as in, 'None of the sand is wet.' A singular verb is also used when one can be interpreted as 'not one' or 'no one' e.g. 'None of us was aware of the problem.' A plural verb is used when none means, 'not any of a group of persons or things.'

Split Infinitive – Strong criticism has been levelled by grammatical purists at anything coming between 'to' and the verb. Today this is regarded as a cramping rule, increasing the difficulty of writing clearly and making for ambiguity.

'That' and 'Which' when used as relative pronouns introducing clauses are often interchangeable, such as 'There's the car that/which had the accident.'

'Though' and 'Although' – usually interchangeable, with 'though' being the more colloquial form: 'I went to the party (al)though I wasn't well.'

Bibliography
and Additional Reading

Bolger, Dermot, ed. *The Picador Book of Contemporary Irish Fiction*. London: Picador, 1993.

Conroy, Róisín, *So You Want to Be Published?* Dublin: Attic Press, 1992.

Crofts, Andrew. *How to Make Money from Freelance Writing*. London: Piatkus, 1992.

Dick, Jill. *Freelance Writing for Newspapers*. London: A and C Black, 1991.

Gowers, Sir Ernest. *ABC of Plain Words*. London: His Majesty's Stationery Office, 1951.

Gunther, Max. *Writing and Selling a Non-Fiction Book*. Boston: The Writer Inc., 1973.

Longmate, Norman. *Writing for the BBC*. London: BBC, 1988.

Prone, Terry. *Write and Get Paid for It*. Dublin: Poolbeg Press, 1989.

St John Thomas, David. *Non-Fiction, A Guide to Writing and Publishing*. London: David and Charles, 1970.

Summers, Vivian. *Clear English*. Harmondsworth, Penguin, 1991.

The Writers' & Artists' Yearbook (1994), A & C Black, London, 1994.